MARCO POLO
SOUTHWESTERN USA

with Local Tips
*The author's special recommendations are
highlighted in yellow throughout this guide*

D1157791

There are five symbols to help you find your way around this guide:

Marco Polo's top recommendations — the best in each category

sites with a scenic view

where the local people meet

where young people get together

(100/A1)
pages and coordinates for the road atlas of the Southwest

MARCO ⊕ POLO

Travel guides and language guides in this series:

Algarve • Amsterdam • Australia • Berlin • Brittany • California
Channel Islands • Costa Brava/Barcelona • Costa del Sol/Granada
Côte d'Azur • Crete • Cuba • Cyprus • Eastern USA • Florence • Florida
Gran Canaria • Greek Islands/Aegean • Ibiza • Ireland • Istanbul • Lanzarote
London • Mallorca • Malta • New York • New Zealand • Normandy • Paris
Prague • Rhodes • Rome • Scotland • South Africa • Southwestern USA
Tenerife • Turkish Coast • Tuscany • Venice • Western Canada

French • German • Italian • Spanish

*Marco Polo would be very interested to hear your
comments and suggestions. Please write to:*

North America:
Marco Polo North America
70 Bloor Street East
Oshawa, Ontario, Canada
(B) 905-436-2525

United Kingdom:
World Leisure Marketing Ltd
Marco Polo Guides
Newmarket Drive
Derby DE24 8 NW

*Our authors have done their research very carefully, but should any errors or omissions
have occurred, the publisher cannot be held responsible for any injury, damage
or inconvenience suffered due to incorrect information in this guide*

Cover photograph: Utah, Glen Canyon, Bridge over the Colorado River (Tony Stone: Schnetz)
Photos: author (7, 26, 28, 33, 68, 83); Frangenberg (24); Hackenberg (15, 18, 38, 66, 86);
HB Verlag, Hamburg (10, 16, 22, 34, 37, 44, 48, 53, 57, 61, 63, 71, 77);
Janicke (80); Layda (4, 54); Mauritius: Hubatka (99); Timmermann (51)

1ˢᵗ edition 1999
© Mairs Geographischer Verlag, Ostfildern, Germany
Author: Karl Teuschl
Translation: Joan Clough
English edition 1999: Gaia Text
Editorial director: Ferdinand Ranft
Chief editor: Marion Zorn
Cartography Road Atlas: © Rand McNally, Chicago; Hallwag AG, Bern
Design and layout: Thienhaus/Wippermann
Printed in Germany

CONTENTS

Discover the Southwest!

Canyons and cacti, Wild West towns and superb resort hotels —
the Southwest really has it all

Since John Ford filmed his classic Western *Ringo* in Monument Valley in 1939, the American Southwest has been making cinematic history. Countless other Westerns were to follow *Ringo* and later there were Road Movies like *Easy Rider* and *Thelma & Louise*. The red mesas, the spectacular canyons and lonely deserts have always been a perfect backdrop for film heroes roaming the classic American Wild West country on horseback in search of freedom and adventure.

This is Route 66 country, crossed by the world's most famously romantic highway to adventure. In the 1930s migrants trooped west on Route 66 yearning for a better life in California. Less than a century ago, Billy the Kid, Butch Cassidy and the Sundance Kid were riding the range in the Southwest. Gold prospectors made boom towns grow up

The road leads straight to Monument Valley, a hallowed shrine for Western fans

over night on this stony soil, trappers and cowboys roamed at will through wild scenery — although they certainly weren't leading the romantic lives cigarette advertisements would have us think.

However, leaving the pioneer sagas and Route 66 nostalgia aside for a moment, the American Southwest is matchless as a place to spend the perfect holiday. Spectacular natural wonders like the Grand Canyon and many other national parks, an arid, nearly always sunny climate and superb infrastructure make the region ideal for holiday-making. A vast region, inhabited by only about 12 million people.

The classic Southwest comprises four states: Arizona and New Mexico to the south, Utah and Colorado to the north. The fantastic gambling paradise of Las Vegas, Nevada, is an honorary member of this Gang of Four, an ideal point of departure for touring throughout the Southwest. The rugged, rocky desert landscape of the Southwest is bounded on the east by the steep green slopes of the Rocky Mountains, and the Sierra Nevada Range separates it from California to the west. The Colorado Plateau forms the heart of the region, a vast bulk of stone thrown up when the continental tectonic plates shifted 60 million years ago. Over millions of years, rivers, wind and weather have carved spectacular gorges in the soft stone. In northern Arizona and southern Utah these geological formations are protected as natural monuments in a host of magnificent national parks: Grand Canyon, Zion, Bryce Canyon, Capitol Reef, Canyonlands and, not least of all these wonders, the fabulous Arches National Park with its grotesque natural arches of red sandstone.

The Colorado Plateau abuts to the south on the vast Sonora Desert, which stretches all the way from the arid basin that is central Arizona as far east as the glittering snow-white gypsum dunes of White Sands National Monument. Around Tucson, Arizona, especially, the desert is at its most capriciously bountiful: winter rains and summer thunderstorms bring enough moisture to sustain uniquely diverse flora, including endless stands of weird cactus. It is only partly true that the further south you go, the hotter it gets. The broad plains are interspersed with mountain ranges, which make temperatures surprisingly cool and pleasant. These mountain ranges are outliers of the Rockies: tranquil, green, cool oases in the shimmering heat of the desert.

Its natural beauty is not the only fascinating thing about the Southwest. The people who live there are a variegated patchwork quilt of three totally different cultures. A thousand years ago the sophisticated Anasazi and Hohokam Cultures flourished here, Indian civilisations that planted corn and built pueblo cities into canyon walls. Their traditions have been preserved by the Pueblo tribes on the Rio Grande and the Hopi Indians of Arizona. Today the Southwest boasts America's largest Indian reservations. Even if modern life has made inroads on the ancient hogans and adobe villages, a strong sense of cultural identity has remained.

The first Europeans came to the region in 1540: Spanish errant knights and missionaries who were to conquer the land in the name of the Church and the Spanish Crown. During the three centuries that followed they founded colonial towns and missions. Even though they were finally driven out, there is to this day a strong Spanish and Mexican feeling about most of New Mexico. The Hispanic influence is in fact growing in the Southwest, for in the past few decades the number of Mexican immigrants who cross the border, which is guarded only by cacti, has continued to increase.

From 1848 Anglo-Americans were the new masters of the Southwest. This marked the dawn of the wildest era of the Wild West: gunslingers robbed prospectors of their gold, bandits attacked post coaches, cattle rustlers made ranchers' lives hell. The US Cavalry relentlessly subdued the last of the free Indian tribes in fierce battles and forced them to live on reservations: the bitter

Vestiges of the Wild West: working cowboys near Telluride, Colorado

memory of this defeat lingers on for Navajos and Apaches. After a long period of suppression, Native American culture has benefited from new attitudes in the past decades. Today, Native Americans are treated with respect; their traditions, symbols and languages are studied by committed anthropologists and archaeologists. Special *tribal taxes* are levied to support the largely autonomous settlement areas where Native Americans are becoming increasingly entrepreneurial in launching their own tourist infrastructure with hotels and casinos.

The white settlers in the Southwest are doing even better than the Native Americans. These latecomers feel thoroughly at home in the desert, braving the rigours of Nature replete with air-conditioned houses, swimming pools and golf courses. Of course, without modern technology, including vast man-made reservoirs and good irrigation fa-

cilities, this sun-scorched region could hardly sustain human life. But the way things are now, this is a great place to live. The Southwest has become fashionable, with the highest population increase in the US. Las Vegas is the biggest success story. Its vast artificial microcosms are by now more than just a gambling paradise; they are an ideal place to marvel at the unlimited American imagination.

Whether you're a Western fan, love nature or are looking for adventure, if you follow the call of the wild *to go West* and head to the Southwest, you'll find it easy to explore: excellent highways, clean motels and superbly sited campgrounds. Take the time to drive aimlessly around on back roads through the interior of this vast country. Many of its natural wonders are not in the famous national parks but are out there waiting for you to discover them and be inspired with awe by their natural grandeur.

History at a glance

After 28,000 BC
Successive waves of migration during the last Ice Age bring Palaeo-Indians from Siberia across the Bering Strait to settle in America

1000-1280 BC
The acme of the Pueblo Cultures: Mogollons, Hohokams and Anasazis build cities, establish farms and make richly ornate pottery

about AD 1400
While the traditional farming tribes like the Hopis and the Pueblos have been sedentary for a long time, nomadic tribes like the Navajos and the Apaches invade the Southwest from the north

after 1538
Spanish expeditions from Mexico explore the south of the region: Francisco Coronado explores New Mexico, López de Cárdenas discovers the Grand Canyon in 1540

about 1600
The Spanish begin to colonize New Mexico, and teach christianity. Santa Fe is founded in 1610

1680
The Pueblos along the Rio Grande revolt. They drive the Spaniards out of New Mexico for 12 years

1776
The US declares its independence. The Spaniards renew their efforts to colonize the Southwest and establish missions in the California Territory

about 1820
US trappers and fur traders like Jedediah Smith head west, crossing the Rocky Mountains. William Becknell is the first US fur trader to reach the colony of New Mexico (1821), now part of the independent state of Mexico, by taking the Santa Fe Trail

1847
The Mormons, persecuted in Illinois, settle in what is now the state of Utah. After losing a war with the US, Mexico is forced to cede its colonies in the Southwest to the US

after 1849
Finds of gold and silver entice pioneers to join the Gold Rush to California (1849), Colorado (1858) and Nevada (1859). Provisions for the *miners* have to be transported by stagecoach. Roads and ranches are built. This is the heyday of the Wild West

1864
The US Cavalry commanded by Colonel Kit Carson quells the Navajo Rebellion. The surviving Navajos are forced to march to New Mexico, where they are banished to a reservation

12 May 1869
The Transcontinental Railroad is finished. The same year John Wesley Powell is the first to go through the Grand Canyon

1881
The Wild West's wildest year: Sheriff Pat Garrett shoots Billy the Kid, New Mexico's most famous gunslinger, on 14 July. On 26 October Marshal Wyatt Earp and Doc Holliday shoot it out with the Clinton Gang in the O.K. Corral at Tombstone in Arizona's most famous gunfight.

1886
After five years of guerilla warfare, the legendary Apache chief, Geronimo, surrenders: the Indian Wars are finally over

1896
After the Mormons abandon the practice of polygamy, Utah becomes a US federal state

1912
Arizona and New Mexico are made US federal states

1926
Route 66 is inaugurated, 3,600 km (2,232 miles) long and America's first transcontinental highway

The 1930s
During the years of the Depression, thousands of farmers who have lost their land leave Oklahoma and Arkansas to go West. Huge building projects such as the construction of the Hoover Dam, create jobs

1936
The first ski lift is built at Aspen, Colorado. The Rocky Mountains make their modest debut as a winter holiday resort

1941
The US enters World War II. Pilots are trained for combat in the Arizona desert while scientists are tinkering with the atomic bomb in the secret laboratories at Los Alamos

The post-war era
Air conditioning and a booming economy make the Southwest America's fastest growing region

1964
The Glen Canyon Dam is completed. It dams up the waters of the Colorado River to form Lake Powell. Other reservoirs, huge aqueducts such as the Central Arizona Project, and irrigation facilities turn the Arizona desert into fertile, arable land

The 1980s
Boom time in the Southwest: during this decade the population of Arizona grows by 35 per cent to reach 3.6 million and Nevada by 50 per cent to 1.2 million people

1992
The US and Canada sign Nafta (North American Free Trade Agreement) with Mexico, bringing an economic upturn to the cities along the border

1995
Salt Lake City and Park City are designated as the venues of the 2002 Winter Olympics

1996
New records are set: 5.2 million visitors to the Grand Canyon — and more than 100,000 weddings in Las Vegas

From the Anasazis to water shortages

*Important background information
for understanding the region*

Anasazi

'The ancient ones, our ancestors' are what the Navajos call the mysterious people who lived long before they came to the tribal territory they occupy today, in what is known as the Four Corners Region. The Anasazi were the most important prehistoric tribe in the Southwest. Whilst the Hohokam and Mogollon tribes in southern Arizona and New Mexico built stone houses and irrigation canals, the Ansazi even developed road systems and built spectacular cliff dwellings.

Even in pre-Christian times prehistoric tribes were living in the Southwest and planting corn. About AD 500 this civilisation evolved into a basketmaking one, *referred to as Archaic*; from 750 they built their first sandstone dwellings. During the Puebloan II Period (about 1200) they erected the cliff dwellings and multi-storey pueblos for which they are famous, notably those in

Tesuque Pueblo: powwows and ceremonies keep Native American traditions alive

Mesa Verde National Park and Chaco Canyon.

About 1280, during a 20-year drought, the Anasazi suddenly abandoned their cliff dwellings and vanished without trace; presumably they intermarried with the ancestors of the Pueblos and Hopis. Moreover, recent research suggests that the Anasazi tribe themselves were the cause of their decline by cutting down the forests on their mesas and thus causing severe erosion: an early example of what unwitting environmental damage can do.

Architecture

Of course the centres of the region's modern metropolises bristle with glass towers and concrete office buildings. However, an unsual number of stylistic elements derived from Native American and early Spanish architecture have moulded the local modern architecture. Pueblo architecture is particularly typical of the region: earth-coloured adobe bricks with rounded corners and the characteristic *vigas,* transverse beams that support flat roofs. They are

11

often only imitations but nevertheless attractive.

Yet there are more than enough historic buildings: the magnificent Mission churches or the ancient pueblos on the Rio Grande. The Western mining towns from the Gold Rush era are quite something else again. Many of them are in Colorado: Victorian architecture with pointed gables, bay windows and gingerbread verandas.

The Southwest also boasts a wealth of modern architecture. Around Santa Fe numerous houses attest to alternative lifestyles. Near Tucson Biosphere 2 will test living on other planets. Architects such as Paolo Soleri and Antoine Predock, are working on pathbreaking projects. The great Frank Lloyd Wright exerted a powerful influence for 20 years from Taliesin West, a camp he founded in 1927 near Phoenix.

Flora and fauna

The Sonora Desert in southern Arizona has enormous species diversity and is one of the world's most fascinating deserts. Violent thunderstorms in summer and occasional winter storms provide enough moisture to sustain biodiversity. About 30 species of cactus grow here. This is the habitat of numerous animal species, many of them nocturnal, like kangaroo rats, coyotes, rattlesnakes, owls and bats. The most remarkable cactus is the Saguaro, which clothes the hills with its picturesquely branching arms familiar from Westerns. These green giants can attain a height of 15 metres (49 ft) and live for 200 years.

The Colorado Plateau, at a higher elevation, is mainly steppe, overgrown with juniper bushes and sagebrush, *Artemisia tridentata*. The canyon beds are often shady green oases and the mountain chains in the region are forested with firs, providing a habitat for deer, mountain lions and even the occasional American bison. The Colorado Rockies are definitively cooler and greener. Their high mountain forests strongly resemble the Alps, with similar flora. Only the names differ: the Rocky Mountain Columbine and the Indian Paint Brush for example.

Geology

The Colorado Plateau (100,000 sq km/38,610 sq miles) forms the heart of the Southwest. More than 1.6 billion years ago a mountain range stood where the plateau now is. It gradually wore down and over aeons fresh layers of sediment, shell limestone and sandstone were added to the bed of what was a shallow inland sea.

Dinosaurs drowned in the swamps bordering the inland sea and were trapped in the sediment. Thick layers of salt and coal developed.

Only about 30 to 60 million years ago, during the same period as the Rocky Mountains emerged, the entire region rose by more than 4,000 m (13,124 ft). When this happened, the vast floor broke up into irregularly shaped plates, which shifted and tilted. The work of erosion began on their edges and on the collision zones: for 10 million years rivers like the Colorado have been cutting ever deeper (1.5 km/

1 mile) into the soft stone, which is brightly coloured by minerals. Wind and frost have shaped grotesque columnar rock formations, stone arches and steep cliffs; the fantastic realm of the canyons was born.

Geronimo

The name of the famous Apache chief symbolizes Native American resistance in the Southwest against the relentless forward march of European civilisation. For over 20 years he fought an exemplary guerilla war against the settlers and the US Cavalry in the mountains of southern Arizona: the last Native American uprising against their conquerors. Geronimo was at times chased by as many as 5,000 US soldiers, yet, brilliant guerilla fighter that he was, he always managed to escape with his Chiricahua warriors. Finally, in 1886 he made his last stand with 36 warriers. After that, Geronimo lived on an Oklahoma reservation until 1909 when, at the age of eighty, he died, falling off a wagon.

History of the political system

The colonial era lasted for nearly 250 years. The scattered settlements along the Rio Grande and in Arizona were at first under Spanish rule and then, from 1821, Mexican. In 1848 the US took over the region, first as a territory administered by the US Army. When the number of settlers grew, the individual regions were changed into federal states. This explains the political structure as it exists today. The Native American reservations, some of them extremely large, have spe-cial status: they are administered autonomously and have their own police. Native Americans on reservations do not have to pay federal and state income tax.

Mormons

A large per cent of the citizens in Utah are Mormons. Mormons frown on drinking and smoking, and attending church on Sundays is a sacred duty. Tithing is strictly practised. The Mormons call themselves the Church of Jesus Christ of Latter-Day Saints. Today they are both a powerful church and an enormously rich business conglomerate with assets totalling well over 15 billion dollars.

Joseph Smith, a New York state farmer's son, founded the Mormon Church. An angel revealed to him a book of the Bible that had been lost. On it he built up his doctrines. After persecution in Illinois led to Smith's death, the Mormons followed their new leader, Brigham Young, westward. The arduous Morman Trail led them to Utah, where they founded Salt Lake City in 1847 as the Jerusalem of the theocratic state of Deseret. They irrigated the desert to make it arable and settled the entire surrounding region. However, not until the Council of Elders agreed to abolish polygamy, which Washington had prohibited, was Utah made a US federal state in 1891.

National parks

When the US Congress designated the geysers of the Yellowstone volcanic district a national park, the world's first, in 1872, the principal aim was to protect a natural wonder. Many of the later national parks (there are 55 of them by now, 12 in the Southwest alone) owed their creation largely to the breathtaking beauty of their scenery. Since the early days of national parks, the philosophy behind them has changed: now the aim is to keep ecosystems intact so that future generations will be able to enjoy them as they have always been. Therefore, exhibitions and tours guided by Rangers increasingly stress preservation of untouched wilderness.

Still the parks and the equally rigorously protected national monuments are a superb natural setting for visits to the region as well as for hiking in the wilderness. They are among the country's most popular resorts. Some national parks, like the Grand Canyon, are in fact threatened with being loved to death. In national parks it is important to follow the rules so that the natural environment suffers as little as possible. Don't feed the animals and don't break off even as much as a twig from a tree or bush. Don't pick any of the flowers. Camping is only permitted at designated sites. Take the time to really experience these parks! Lookout points may be crowded but a day's walk into the interior will take you far away from it all. Many visitors are elderly people or groups of children who seldom stray far from the lookout points. If you want to visit more than one national park in the course of a holiday, you should buy a Gold Eagle Pass for $50 in the first park you visit. It entitles you to visit all national parks and National Monuments.

Native Americans today

About 100,000 descendants of the First Americans today live in the southwestern states: Tohono O'odham and Apaches in the far south; the Pueblo tribes along the Rio Grande in New Mexico and the Utes, mainly in the state of Utah, which is named after them. The most populous Native American tribe, however, is the Navajo (200,000), the greatest Native American nation in the US. The Navajos own a vast (65,000 sq km/26,000 sq miles) reservation, which they administer almost entirely themselves. The other tribes also all have territories of their own, albeit smaller ones.

By the pioneer era in the 19th century, the Native Americans had been forced to live on reservations, empty tracts of land that the conquerors had not claimed because they were not suitable for ranching and farming. Most native American settlements did not prosper agricuturally and look bleak. Many Native Americans are on welfare, today.

Native American schooling, life expectancy and living standards are far below those of white Americans. Nevertheless, the Indian tribes of the Southwest are more fortunate than their fellows in the east in being able to live on their original tribal lands. This is the reason why they have been able to stay in touch with 'Holy Mother Earth', thus preserving their cultural identity. The Pueblos and the Hopi especially, who have kept themselves apart from White America, have retained their traditional culture and way of life to this day.

A modern hotel in the ancient pueblo style: Loretto Inn, Santa Fe

Population

Desert living is in. Nevada (Las Vegas!) and Arizona regularly head the US population growth tables. The population of Nevada alone grew by 50 per cent between 1980 and 1990. Arizona wasn't far behind with a 35 per cent population growth. Cities like Phoenix are in the throes of a population explosion, which will make them vast metropolises marred by uncontrolled urban sprawl, at no matter what cost to the natural environment.

About 10 million people are already living in these four southwestern states, 70 per cent of them in large cities. Away from the cities, the country is only sparsely populated. About three-quarters of the population are not Native Americans but are descendants of the pioneers who settled the West in the 19th century or have migrated here in the past few decades. There are very few African Americans

here, only between 2 and 6 per cent of the overall population. The Hispanics are the second largest ethnic group. Some are descendants of the early Spanish colonists, but most have immigrated recently from Mexico. The official figures are 18.8 per cent Hispanics in Arizona and 38.2 per cent in New Mexico. Thousands of immigrants cross the border from Mexico daily, often illegally. The 'Tortilla Curtain' is permeable and border police are unable to stop this mass immigration despite fences and regular border checks.

Pueblos

The Native American tribes in northern New Mexico as well as the sophisticated Anasazi culture of the 13th century were named by the Spaniards; *pueblos,* meaning villages, was the term used by the Conquistadores for the Native American settlements along the Rio Grande. The word now stands for the specifically Indian style of architecture. Roughly hewn sandstone blocks and sun-dried mud bricks *(adobe)* were used from about AD 900 by Indian tribes in the Four Corners Region to build large domestic settlements – you might call them prehistoric high-rise flat blocks. Some, like Taos Pueblo, are up to five storeys high. There are still about 25 pueblos in New Mexico. Each of them has the traditional living quarters, storerooms and *kivas,* round, subterranean ceremonial rooms.

Resources and economy

Before 1930, mining and cattle ranching were the traditional pillars of the economy in the southwestern states. Today they are no longer as important as they once were, but they continue to play a role in the regional economy: coal, uranium and copper are still mined and herds of cattle graze the Colorado valleys. Agriculture started growing on a large scale in the

1930's after large reservoirs and extensive irrigation canals were built. After World War II other industries became established: armaments factories, food-processing plants, the electronics and computer industry. Banks and insurance companies have moved into the sunny Southwest. In recent decades tourism has contributed heavily to economic growth in the region, especially in Arizona and Las Vegas, the gambling paradise.

Rodeos

Rodeos are by far the most popular public events in the Southwest. What used to be informal cowboy events has grown into a professional, albeit still pretty rugged, sports. Places like Payson, Prescott or Durango stage rodeos every couple of weeks. In many smaller towns public rough riding on bucking broncos takes place at least once a year. Cowboys come from as far away as Canada and Australia to participate in the big champion-

Broken bones and all: bull riding is considered the most dangerous rodeo event

ship rodeos put on in Las Vegas and Phoenix. Tough guys take a broken rib as all part of the day's work. Champions can win up to $20,000.

The most important rodeo events are: *Bareback Riding* or *saddle bronco riding,* where the cowboy has to stay on a wildly bucking bronco for at least eight seconds. *Bull riding* is just what the name implies, in this event riders have to stick on the back of an enraged bull for eight seconds or more. Other events, like *steer wrestling* or *calf roping,* require participants to lasso (whilst riding a galloping horse) a young bull or a calf, which they then have to wrestle to the ground. Certainly not an easy task either.

Snowbirds

'Snowbirds' is the local term for the (usually elderly) refugees from the winter snows of Canada and the Midwest. Every year in November they descend on sunny Arizona like swarms of migratory birds. They stay over the winter, some drive through the countryside in luxuriously equipped super caravans (trailers), others prefer to rent holiday flats, which are invariably close to swimming pools and golf courses. Many old-age pensioners from the northern states have elected to settle permanently in these milder climates, especially Arizona, where they can enjoy a sunny old age. Entire pensioner settlements, for example 'Sun City' near Phoenix, have been built to cater for these elderly sun-seekers. And you only qualify as a buyer if you're over 50 years old.

Water shortage

The average resident of desert cities like Las Vegas or Phoenix may use anywhere from 800 to 1,000 litres (176 to 220 gallons) of water a day — for swimming pools, dishwasher, showers, washing machines, watering the garden or even irrigating the nearby golf course. That's a high price to pay for a pleasant life warmed by eternal sun when you consider that the average Central European only uses between 80 and 100 litres (18 to 22 gallons) of water a day. Rivers like the Colorado or the Rio Grande are swollen in spring with melt water from the Rocky Mountains, yet they are being drained dry. More than 20 dams block the 2,300 km (1,426 mile)-long course of the Colorado River and its tributaries. The waters of the Colorado River system no longer reach the Gulf of California because they have been used into irrigated fields and fill the many swimming pools. The large Central Arizona Project aqueduct, finished in 1991, now brings precious water to Tucson from Colorado, 500 km (310 miles) away.

In the meantime, dire forecasts for the future are the order of the day: the ground water is rapidly being depleted, the large reservoirs are slowly but surely silting up and extreme evaporation is actually changing the desert climate. Man's ill-considered encroachment on the natural environment is exacting a heavy toll indeed as the price for air-conditioned living in the desert and also the thirst of the sprawling cities seems unquenchable.

Cowboy chow and margaritas

Steaks belong to the Southwest like cactus to the desert, but there are lots of other good things to eat

The Southwest is cowboy country. And cowboys spend their lives eating the animals they herd all day. Right? Not really. If you really don't like steak, you'll find plenty of other delicious things to eat in the Southwest. Those who spurn steaks will probably only be regarded as slightly loco in small towns way out in the boondocks — unless they decide on *prime rib,* a thick juicy slice of rare rib roast of beef (not to be confused with marinated, grilled *spare ribs*). In any case, portions are hearty and main courses *(entrées)* come with side dishes (usually vegetables and a *baked potato*) as well as soup or a salad for starters; sometimes both are included.

However, no one who eschews steak will die of starvation. Every major highway intersection has burger stops and all medium size towns boast Mexican, Italian, Chinese and fastfood restaurants (Pizza Hut, Taco Bell, Subway, Denny's). Big cities abound in Japanese, Arab, Caribbean, Indian and French

A big, juicy steak? Coming right up!

cuisine, soul food prepared by immigrants from around the world and available at any price you're prepared to pay.

Runny, stringy cheese is a feature of some Mexican specialities and spruces up many a US classic, such as sandwiches, burgers and pizza: stop worrying about cholesterol and tuck into a lavish *American breakfast* with fried eggs to start the day. You can order *health food* instead, with muesli *(granola),* oatmeal *(porridge),* granary bread *(wholegrain)* and even salads. Speaking of breakfast: the cheapest buffet breakfast spreads are served at the Las Vegas casino hotels. In many other places room prices now include a light breakfast.

Drinks
Ice water is always served but you might like to try a beer to quench your thirst after a long and hot day's travelling. It's not very strong. Mexican brands (Corona, Dos Equis) taste more like European beer. The latest fad here is something America has only recently launched: *microbreweries,* which are small

breweries belonging to one particular restaurant. Cowboy country is now enjoying top-brewed beer on Bavarian lines. However, watch out for *root beer,* which is dark and cloyingly sweet, a soft drink that tastes like chewing gum.

Wine drinkers can choose California vintages (white Chardonnays, fruity red Zinfandels, Cabernets etc) but these are sometimes world-class wines and therefore often expensive. New Mexico has also taken to producing wine in recent years.

An icy margarita in a salt-rimmed daiquiri glass (great for making up salt lost from sweating!) is the typical Southwest aperitif, but you'll usually find a wide range of other *mixed drinks* made with tequila, rum, bourbon or Scotch in all bars.

Restaurants

Breakfast is usually served in coffee shops. They may be part of a hotel or are located near a motel. Once there, you can choose between a light *continental breakfast* (juice, coffee, toast and marmalade) or splurge on a hearty *American breakfast,* which will stick to your ribs all day. It includes eggs (*sunny-side up* = fried eggs, *over-easy* = flipped over, *scrambled* = per usual, *boiled* = soft or hard), bacon *(streaky)* or ham *(lean)* and even fried potatoes *(hash browns)* as well as toast and marmalade. Treat yourself to *French toast* or an omelette, fluffy or otherwise.

Lunch, usually served between 12 and 2 pm, is not a big meal in the US. Americans prefer a light meal at noon, with a separate menu *(lunch menu),* which may include: *Caesar salad* or *soup and sandwich.* You may also be tempted by a generous salad bar buffet lunch or even a hamburger. Some of these can be surprisingly good if made to order.

The evening meal *(dinner)* is served in rural areas between 6 and 7 pm, in cities between 7 and 10 pm. As in the rest of America, it is not uncommon to queue up for a table. A sign at the entrance says: *Please wait to be seated.* Smoking, if it is allowed at all, is only permitted in separate rooms of larger restaurants.

Southwest cuisine

In Santa Fe, Taos, Tucson and Phoenix/Scottsdale an imaginative new style of cooking has developed under the name of Southwest cuisine. In New Mexico it has mainly been inspired by Mexican and Native American cooking. Arizona cooking leans more towards the California cuisine style, which startled the gourmet world in the 1970s. Creative chefs from all over the world joined US traditionalists to produce superb eclectic fare and imaginative, often bold, combinations ranging from fruit with meat to the more standard creations of Asian and Mexican cuisine.

The new Southwest style of cooking is light and utilizes fresh regional produce: pine kernels or such delights as slices of cactus fruit on salads, Native American piki bread made of blue corn (maize) as a side dish, pumpkin and all sorts of bean and of course fiery hot chili peppers, a legacy of the Spaniards who colonized the Southwest.

Outlet malls and trading posts

Traditional Native American crafts are popular souvenirs, but there's much, much more to buy

Shopping is a favourite pastime in the US. Therefore, customer convenience has been given top priority: purchasers of any goods may use their credit cards to the limit. Shops are very well stocked and personnel is chosen for helpfulness and politeness. When you enter a boutique, you are greeted with *Hi, can I help you?* At many supermarkets a person awaits you after you've paid at the cashier. He or she will carefully 'bag' your purchases and even carry everything to your car. The service is mostly very good.

In larger cities shoppers gravitate towards vast — invariably air-conditioned — shopping malls comprising 100 or more shops, department store retail outlets and restaurants. Some of these malls, like Trolley Square in Salt Lake City, are housed in historic buildings; others are postmodern complexes like the Arizona Center in Phoenix. Shopping is a prime leisure activity in America. Malls are where people meet to pass the time of day with family and friends. Outlet malls are the newest trend. These are shopping complexes where brand-name articles like Levis, Nike and Samsonite luggage are sold at factory discounts. These cheap factory outlets are usually well out of town on highways, where rents are lower and overhead costs can be kept at a minimum.

Consumer goods are cheap in the US, even if you may have to take a higher exchange rate for the dollar into consideration. You'll still be amazed at how much cheaper casual clothing like jeans, sportswear, sport footwear and sporting goods are than at home. Costume jewellery and even designer fashions are often a better buy than in other countries. Sales seem to be on all year round in large department stores and mall retail outlets. However, once you leave the beaten track for the open country, things look very different. Rural areas are adequately stocked with basic commodities, yet there isn't much of a selection of goods to choose from. A small retail store *(general store),* which sells not only food staples but everything imaginable from gasoline and fishing tackle to spades and other tools, is often the only place to shop in small Utah and New Mexican towns.

An ancient Navajo craft: weaving wool rugs

Native American art and Western wear

Among the loveliest souvenirs you can take home from the Southwest are Native American crafts, which are sold at many galleries, museum shops and trading posts on and near Indian reservations. The Navajos, for example, make silver jewellery and woollen blankets, raising the sheep from whose wool they weave the blankets. They also make sand pictures, 'paintings' of ancient symbols in multi-coloured sand, traditionally used by medicine men to heal the sick. The Zuni tribe is famous for turquoise, coral and mother of pearl intarsia work. And the Pueblos along the Rio Grande are renowned for their ceramics. Each pueblo has developed its own distinctive style: at Acoma pottery is decorated with geometric patterns; the inhabitants of Santa Clara Pueblo make hand-polished black ceramics and at the Cochiti Pueblo you'll find the famous storyteller figures. Hot collector's items are the *kachinas* made by the Hopi: marvellously decorated wooden dolls, which the Hopi used to carve for their children to make them familiar with the spirit world. Nowadays these figures cost upwards of $300.

However, there are many more – and much cheaper – articles you can shop for in the Southwest such as Western or cowboy outfits: Stetson hats, hand-made cowboy boots or silver belt buckles. In most cities you'll find shops selling *Western wear.* Local produce and preserves also make very attractive souvenirs: Arizona cactus marmalade, hot New Mexico salsa or Colorado wild-flower honey. Be careful with cacti. These spiny plants populate the southern Arizona desert but they're not up for grabs. They are protected by law. Taking shoots from them is prohibited.

Many visitors to the Southwest swear by Native American crafts. Of course there's a lot of junk on sale as well: Western kitsch landscapes in oils or romantic plaster figures of Indian chiefs that look like miniature tobacco-store Indians. Nonetheless, there are many lovely and authentic hand crafted things to buy, especially in Santa Fe, Taos and Sedona. Since the painter Georgia O'Keeffe settled on the Rio Grande in this century, many artists have followed in her footsteps, inspired by the superb Southwest scenery. There are dozens of art galleries that line Canyon Road in Santa Fe, some of them selling excellent work.

Sizes

During the 1970s, the US tried to convert to the metric system, but the attempt was so unpopular that it failed. Consequently, you still buy clothing and shoes in American sizes. T-shirts and Western shirts come in *small, medium, large* and *X-tra large.* Be careful when buying dresses or trousers off the peg. US women's size 4 corresponds to British women's 34, 6 = 36, 8 = 38, 10 = 40 and so on. Men's sizes follow a similar scale: US men's size 36 corresponds to 46, 38 = 48, 40 = 50 etc. When in doubt, always ask and you'll always find a friendly salesperson willing to oblige with a tape-measure.

Art markets and tribal dancing

*Every city and village throws a pioneer festival once a year —
usually with a fair and a big rodeo*

A host of festivals throughout the year keep the memory of the pioneer era alive in the Southwest. Mock gunfights with blank cartridges and costume parades, beauty pageants, rodeos and jamborees commemorate pioneer, cowboy and Gold Rush days in the Wild West. Moreover, you shouldn't miss the Indian tribal festivals, which centre on dancing in colourful costume. Navajo dance groups from across the US converge on Navajo reservations for big powwows. You may even have the honour of being permitted to watch ceremonial dancing at festivals held in the pueblos along the Rio Grande.

In addition to Native American and Western cultural events, you'll find the calendar packed with numerous other occasions for celebration: mountain bike and jeep rallies; craft fairs where Indian work and modern Southwest crafts are sold; music fes tivals featuring Country and Western, Bluegrass and Jazz;

*Bright confetti above the desert:
Albuquerque Balloon Fiesta*

Mexican fiestas and even highly enjoyable chili con carne cooking contests. Wherever you are, just ask at your local Visitor Center. There's sure to be something scheduled for the following weekend.

Religious festivals are not publicly emphasized in the US as they are in continental European countries. In American cities, shops are usually open on Easter and even on Christmas Day. State holidays are traditionally on a Monday to extend the weekend, which gives people a chance to take a short break. Two such weekends frame the summer peak holiday season: Memorial Day weekend at the end of May marks the beginning of the summer season, which closes with Labor Day weekend at the beginning of September.

OFFICIAL HOLIDAYS

Banks, schools, post offices and even many museums are closed on the following holidays:
1 January: *New Year's Day*
Third Monday in January: *Martin Luther King Jr. Day*
Third Monday in February:

Matachina Dance at Santa Clara Pueblo: with historic costumes

President's Day

Last Monday in May: *Memorial Day* (honours war dead)

4 July: *Independence Day* (independence from Britain)

24 July: *Pioneer Day* (in Utah)

First Monday in August: *Colorado Day* (in Colorado)

First Monday in September: *Labor Day* (honours working people)

Second Monday in October: *Columbus Day*

11 November: *Veterans' Day*

Fourth Thursday in November: *Thanksgiving Day*

EVENTS

February

Crested Butte, CO: the month begins with the exciting *Extreme Skiing Championships,* with expert skiers racing headlong downhill. Parties and parades.

Tucson, AZ: late in February the *Fiesta de los vaqueros* commemorates the founding of the city by Mexico with equine events and big parades.

March

Phoenix, AZ: *Indian Fair and Market* in the Heard Museum; one of the best venues for buying Native American art. In early March.

Easter is celebrated in many Rio Grande pueblos with *ceremonial dances* in advance.

May

❂ *Cinco de Mayo,* Mexican Independence Day, is celebrated in Arizona and New Mexico with fiestas and mariachi bands, fairs and parades over the weekend closest to 5 May.

Tombstone, AZ: at the end of the month gunslingers meet for the Pioneer Festival called *Wyatt Earp Day.*

June

Payson, AZ: ★ *Junior Rodeo* mid-June

Telluride, CO: *Bluegrass Festival.* For four days in mid-month, America's best Country and Western fiddlers meet and compete.

★ *San Juan Feast Day* 24 June: Ceremonial dancing in the Cochiti, Taos and Acoma Pueblos.

July

❂ *Fourth of July:* the American national holiday is celebrated with passionate patriotism, especially in small Southwestern towns like Prescott, Durango and Aspen. Colourful parades, barbecues and, of course, firework displays.

Payson, AZ: the *Loggers' Sawdust Festival* in mid-month finds Arizona loggers swinging their axes.

Logan, UT: the Mormon Trail is re-created; Country and Western music and a fair celebrate the ★ *Festival of the American West,* reviving the pioneer era in the northern Utah mountains.

August
Gallup, NM: the *Inter-Tribal Indian Ceremonial,* the Southwest's biggest Native American festival is held during the second week of this month.

Santa Fe, NM: in mid-August *the Indian Market,* the oldest Native American art market in the US, is held.

September
Window Rock, NM: the month begins with the *Navajo Nation Fair,* tribal dances (powwow) with a rodeo and Miss Navajo election.

Bonneville Salt Flats, UT: the world's fastest cars race through the salt flats near Salt Lake City in the *World of Speed Races* to set new records.

Taos, NM: at the *Feast of San Geronimo* at the end of the month, the inhabitants of Taos Pueblo stage ceremonial dances and a pole-shinning contest.

October
Albuquerque, NM: for a whole week early in the month, the ★ *International Balloon Fiesta* fills the skies with crazy hot air balloons.

Phoenix, AZ: the latter half of the month *Arizona State Fair,* the Southwest's biggest fair with Country and Western music

Moab, UT: the world's best mountain bikers show their stuff at the end of the month at the ⚚ *Fat Tire Festival.*

December
Long before Christmas many towns are decorated with bright garlands of light and stage *Christmas parades.* Notable venues: Santa Fe, Salt Lake City and small Victorian towns in Colorado, such as Telluride and Aspen.

Santa Fe, NM: at Christmastime *dances in many pueblos.*

Phoenix/Tempe, AZ: on New Year's Eve the College Football season ends with the huge *Fiesta Bowl Parade* celebration.

MARCO POLO SELECTION: FESTIVALS

1 Festival of the American West in Logan
A rodeo, a parade and the Morman Trail: a great day for Western fans (page 27)

2 International Balloon Fiesta in Albuquerque
Hot-air balloons float over the New Mexico desert at the world's biggest ballooning event (page 27)

3 Payson Junior Rodeo
Five to eighteen-year-old aficionados show their skills riding on bucking broncos and raging bulls (page 26)

4 San Juan Feast Day
A look at Pueblo Indian life with dances, ceremonies and Native American cooking (page 26)

The desert capital of glitz

Spectacular shows and casinos tricked out in neon:
Las Vegas is the setting for winner takes all

Las Vegas (**105/F2**), a surreal oasis in the southern Nevada desert, is, especially for American gambling aficionados, a wonderland and a fantastic refuge from mundane cares. Like a fascinating dream in technicolour, Las Vegas promises fun and entertainment, maybe even the chance to break the bank. In only 50 years, this

Illusion is everything:
the Luxor Casino is ancient Egypt

remote desert city has mushroomed into the world capital of gambling.

Thirty million visitors come to Las Vegas each year and 6 billion dollars change hands there. New supercasinos, new shows all the time and attractions offered nowhere else in the world draw visitors like a magnet. Round the clock and 365 days a year neon lights flicker, one-armed bandits clatter and roulette balls roll endlessly. Gamblers lose all track of

---

Hotel and restaurant prices

Hotels
Category 1: Luxury hotels and holiday resorts above $130
Category 2: Good hotels, B & Bs and motels below $130
Category 3: Modest motels and B & Bs below $70

Prices are for two people in a double room. Single rooms are not much cheaper. Children can usually sleep free of charge in their parents' room.

Restaurants
Category 1: Above $40
Category 2: From $20 to $40
Category 3: Below $20
Prices are for a three-course evening meal.

Abbreviations
Ave.	Avenue
Blvd.	Boulevard
Dr.	Drive
Hwy.	Highway
Rd.	Road
St.	Street

time and the weather in these air-conditioned dream palaces. Outside in the Nevada desert the sun is always shining anyway. People sleep now and then in Las Vegas, but not long enough to keep them from what they came here for: the chance to win. Las Vegas is for many the chance to see if the American Dream can come true.

The gambling paradise boomed (today the population of the Las Vegas conurbation is 1.2 million) virtually overnight. In 1855 pious Mormons founded the settlement of Las Vegas (Spanish, meaning 'the meadows') in a southern Nevada valley oasis. After the advent of the railroad, it had grown into a small town by about 1910. However, the 1930s saw the first sharp upturn: in 1931 the state of Nevada legalized gambling. Soon afterwards, construction of the Hoover Dam brought an army of labourers (all inveterate gamblers) and cheap electricity. In the 1940s legendary

racketeers like Bugsy Siegel started building the first big casinos along the 'Las Vegas Strip'. Large firms and investment banks later got into the act by putting their stamp of approval on what had by now become big business.

Only once since then, in the late 1980s, has Lady Luck seemed to desert her favourite haunts. At that time casinos were being built throughout America. Who needed Las Vegas now? However, that old gambling instinct paid off and the city rejuvenated itself. In record time enormous new fantasy palaces and theme parks shot up from the desert sand. Large-scale projects are now in the pipeline: attractions for children and families, putting greens for golfers, swimming pool complexes for discerning holiday-makers and, of course, newer and bigger casinos.

Las Vegas is fashionable again. A stroll down the 'Strip' is an exhillerating experience on a cos-

MARCO POLO SELECTION: LAS VEGAS

1 Caesars Palace
Almost like ancient Rome: the fountain sculptures even come alive (page 33)

2 Dive!
Dinner in a submarine? Film director Steven Spielberg designed the interior (page 35)

3 Hoover Dam
Man-made grandeur: the raging Colorado River is harnessed in Black Canyon (pages 36–37)

4 New York-New York
The city's zaniest architecture: a casino that is a replica of the New York skyline (page 36)

5 Star Trek
Beam us up, Scotty! A must for all committed 'Star Trek' aficionados (page 34)

6 Treasure Island
Pirates ahoy! Buccaneers are engaged in sea battles four times a day (page 33)

mic scale: volcanoes spewing fire, medieval castles and Egyptian pyramids vie for your attention with full-sized replicas of famous New York and Paris buildings. Oddly enough, a luxury holiday is really affordable in Las Vegas since hotels, restaurants and shows are all subsidized by the casinos. A sumptuous hotel room, which would set you back $300 anywhere else, costs only $100 here. An elegantly landscaped pool complex in the resort hotel of your choice is simply part of the package, not to mention sunshine all year round. To top it off, an opulent buffet dinner is thrown in for a mere $9.99.

Visitors are meant to find their way to the casinos eventually. Lady Luck exacts her tribute of dollars, whether you're playing blackjack or roulette, twisting the arm of one of 140,000 'one-armed bandits' or simply playing good old American poker. You don't have to know the rules; many casinos offer free instruction in gambling. If you're itching to tie the knot, you can get hitched, as they say in the West, at the drop of a hat in Las Vegas, at 3 am in one of the *wedding chapels*, which are open for weddings round the clock. You can have all the pomp and ceremony you want in any one of a myriad chapels or simply get into your car and drive to a *drive-up window* — as your heart desires.

A wedding night for just the two of you isn't on in Las Vegas because shows, themed restaurants and bars tempt honeymooners before they even think of bed. Casinos can afford entertainers like Liza Minnelli, Sieg-

fried & Roy or Diana Ross. Glamorous Paris revues and technicolour shows like the 'Cirque du Soleil' lend a touch of European savoir vivre. Las Vegas does everything to keep the dollars rolling.

SIGHTS

You definitely should plan to spend at least one or two days seeing some of the gigantic casinos and other Las Vegas attractions. The best thing to do is spend your days at the pool or undertake day trips in the surrounding desert. It's only at night, when the whole city is ablaze with neon lights, that its bizarre beauty can be fully appreciated.

It isn't hard to find your away around Las Vegas. The casinos are clustered around two hubs, which are only a couple of minutes apart by taxi: the downtown casinos around Fremont Street and the famous Las Vegas Boulevard, called *The Strip.* The older gambling palaces are in the historic downtown section, among them the *Golden Nugget* and the *Four Queens,* all of which had seen better days by the 1980s. Since then, however, millions of dollars have been spent on restoring Fremont Street, which has been roofed over as an open-air theme park.

South of downtown, along the Strip or between Sahara and Tropicana Avenues, the supercasino hotels await your pleasure with shows, waterfalls and fantasy worlds. At the northern end of the Strip, you'll find the older casinos, like *Circus Circus* with acrobats performing on the flying trapeze under a multicoloured dome. Further south, before you

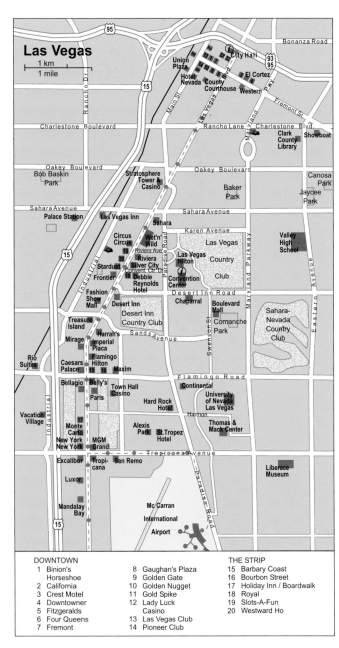

Las Vegas

1 km
1 mile

Bonanza Road

95

City Hall
93
95

Union Plaza
Hotel Nevada
County Courthouse
El Cortez
Western
Fremont St.

15

Main St.

Las Vegas Blvd.

Maryland Pkwy

Charlestone Boulevard
Rancho Lane
Charlestone Blvd.
Clark County Library
Showboat

Oakey Boulevard
Bob Baskin Park
Oakey Boulevard
Canosa Park
Jaycee Park

Stratosphere Tower & Casino
Baker Park

Sahara Avenue
Palace Station
Sahara Avenue
Las Vegas Inn
Sahara
Karen Avenue

Circus Circus
Wet'n' Wild
Riviera Ave.
Riviera
Silver City
Convent. Ctr. Dr.
Las Vegas Country Club
Las Vegas High School
Valley High School

15
Industria
Stardust
Frontier
Debbie Reynolds Hotel
Las Vegas Hilton
Convention Center

Fashion Show Mall
Desert Inn
Desert Inn Road
Chaparral
Desert Inn Country Club
Boulevard Mall
Sahara-Nevada Country Club

Treasure Island
Mirage
Harrah's
Imperial Placa
Sands Avenue
Comanche Park
Eastern Avenue

Rio Suites
Caesars Palace
Flamingo Hilton
Maxim
Flamingo Road

Bellagio
Bally's
Paris
Town Hall Casino
Hard Rock Hotel
Continental
University of Nevada Las Vegas

Vacation Village
Monte Carlo
New York New York
Alexis Park
St.Tropez Hotel
Harmon
Thomas & Mack Center

Excalibur
Tropi-cana
San Remo
MGM Grand
Tropicana Avenue

Luxor
Liberace Museum

Mandalay Bay
15

Mc Carran International Airport

Paradise Road

DOWNTOWN

1 Binion's Horseshoe
2 California
3 Crest Motel
4 Downtowner
5 Fitzgeralds
6 Four Queens
7 Fremont

8 Gaughan's Plaza
9 Golden Gate
10 Golden Nugget
11 Gold Spike
12 Lady Luck Casino
13 Las Vegas Club
14 Pioneer Club

THE STRIP

15 Barbary Coast
16 Bourbon Street
17 Holiday Inn / Boardwalk
18 Royal
19 Slots-A-Fun
20 Westward Ho

reach the dazzling brightness of the Flamingo Road intersection, you'll spot more famous names, like ★ *Treasure Island,* where pirates battle eternally in the Treasure Island lagoon, and next door, the *Mirage Resort,* where an artificial volcano spews fire at night, and, most fabulous of all, *Caesars Palace.* Slightly further south, on the Strip, the spectacular new resorts built in the past few years include the elegant *Bellagio,* the *MGM Grand Hot,* which has its own pleasure grounds and 5,005 rooms, the world's second largest hotel. Then, laid out like a medieval castle, the *Excalibur Casino* and, last but not least, *New York-New York.*

Caesars Palace

★ A total work of art built in 1966, in vaguely Roman style. Lit up turquoise at night and framed by fountains and sculptures, this showy building is the *grande dame* of Las Vegas casinos. It boasts a replica of ancient Rome, movies in an Omnimax film theatre and Forum Shops, a chic shopping arcade under an artificial sky. *3570 Las Vegas Blvd. S*

Fremont Street Experience

Every evening the main street at the heart of Las Vegas is roofed over for five blocks to form a showcase: 2.1 million lightbulbs and huge batteries of loudspeakers create a Brobdingnagian Sound & Light spectacle the year round.

Hard Rock Hotel Casino

🛉 After the Hard Rock Café chain had conquered the world, here's the hotel that belongs to it: decorated with rock memorabilia and host to rock stars every evening on the vast stage of the *Joint* in the hotel. *4475 Paradise Rd.*

Luxor

A pyramid of dark glass, guarded by a Sphinx and, at 100 m (328 ft), higher than anything on the Nile. Inside it you can gape at the Pharaoh Tutankhamen's

Roman sculptures for a temple of Mammon: Caesars Palace Casino in all its glory

treasures. The lobby, which is 30 storeys high, is graced by an obelisk. *3900 Las Vegas Blvd. S*

Star Trek – The Experience
★ No lesser beings than Mr Spock and Captain Kirk have had suites at the Las Vegas Hilton since January 1998.
Daily 11 am–11 pm; Admission: $14.95; 3000 Paradise Rd.

Stratosphere Tower
〰 America's highest lookout tower (350 m, 1,148 ft) is the newest landmark on the Las Vegas skyline. At the very top a roller-coaster hurtles headlong into outer space. There are also three wedding chapels at the top, and for the less adventurous, a bar and a restaurant. *2000 Las Vegas Blvd. S*

Imperial Palace Auto Collection
A delight for connoisseurs of old cars: on the top floor of the Imperial Palace Hotel about 200 classic cruisers as well as Hitler's very own Daimler and the magnificent coach that belonged to the King of Siam. *Daily 9.30 am–11.30 pm; Admission: $6.95; 3535 Las Vegas Blvd. S*

Most large casino hotels offer very reasonably priced, yet opulent buffet meals. However, since long queues often form at the cheapest buffets, at Circus Circus or in the MGM Grand Hotel, it's advisable to spend a bit more and enjoy a much better buffet at the

Dollars change hands round the clock: one-armed bandits are always insatiable

34

Monte Carlo Casino or Caesars
Palace. In addition, there are coffee shops in all hotels, and most
of them are open round the
clock for breakfast and dinner,
catering for all tastes.

Chinois Las Vegas
A posh hotel for beautiful people. The Austrian star chef Wolf-
gang Puck creates light, imaginative Asian-Californian cuisine.
*Forum Shops in Caesars Palace; 3500
Las Vegas Blvd.; Tel: (702) 737-
9700; Category 2*

Coyote Café
A trendy and popular eatery
serving superb Mexican-inspired
Southwest cuisine. *In the MGM
Grand Hotel; 3799 Las Vegas Blvd.
S; Tel: (702) 891-7777; Category 2*

Dive!
★ A magnificently eccentric res-
taurant decorated like a submar-
ine. For sandwiches and steaks.
*In the Fashion Show Mall; 3200 Las
Vegas Blvd. S; Tel: (702) 369-3483;
Category 2-3*

Kokomo's
Steak and seafood served in the
lush tropics of the Mirage Resort
lobby. *3400 Las Vegas Blvd. S; Tel:
(702) 791-7111; Category 2*

Marie Callenders
☨ Good American home cooking
some distance from the Strip. Excellent pies. *600 E Sahara Ave.;
Tel: (702) 734-6572; Category 2–3*

Wild Bill's
Big juicy steaks in a Western am-
bience and dancing to Country
& Western music. *In the Excalibur
Casino, 3850 Las Vegas Blvd. S;
Tel: (702) 597-7777; Category 2*

Belz Facory Outlet World
Large mall with discount brand-
name articles by Nike, OshKosh,
Danskin and others. *7400 Las
Vegas Blvd. S*

Fashion Show Mall
Elegant shopping centre with
about 130 boutiques and restaurants. *3200 Las Vegas Blvd. S*

There may be smaller motels
in the side streets of Las Vegas
but this is one city in which you
really should splurge on treating
yourself to the occasional night
in one of the casino palaces. At
weekends hotel prices are higher;
from Sunday to Thursday rooms
are considerably cheaper.

Caesars Palace
Ancient Rome sumptuously re-
invented to make this the city's
classic luxury hotel. *3,600 rooms;
3570 Las Vegas Blvd. S; Tel: (702)
731-7110; Fax: 731-6636; Category 1*

Golden Nugget
A celebrated casino hotel right in
the downtown bustle with about
1,900 modern rooms ranging from
moderately priced to expensive.
*129 E Fremont St.; Tel: (702) 385-
7111; Fax: 386-8362; Category 1–3*

Imperial Palace
Comfortable and in a good location on the Strip. *2,700 rooms; 3535
Las Vegas Blvd. S; Tel: (702) 731-
3311; Fax: 735-8578; Category 2–3*

Monte Carlo
A new, very elegant casino hotel
in a prime location on the Strip,

with 6 restaurants and its own brewery on the premises. *3,014 rooms; 3770 Las Vegas Blvd.; Tel: (702) 730-7777; Fax: 730-7250; Category 2*

New York-New York
★ A quick trip to New York? This sparkling new hotel, opened in 1997, makes it possible. *2,035 rooms; 3790 Las Vegas Blvd. S; Tel: (702) 740-6969; Fax: 740-6920; Category 1–2*

SPORTS & LEISURE

Most casino hotels have fitness centres and swimming pools, often set in spacious, landscaped environments. Some even have tennis courts. At the reception desk you can book for a game of golf at one of at least 30 courses in Las Vegas.

Wet 'n' Wild Water Park
Acres and acres of slides and pools with waves – great entertainment value for children. *May–Dec. daily 10 am–6 pm; Admission: $22.95, children $16.95; 2600 Las Vegas Blvd. S*

ENTERTAINMENT

You won't find big-name revues and concerts given by famous performers anywhere else in the US as cheap as they are in Las Vegas. There's usually a dinner performance at about 8 pm for $30 to $60 and a cocktail show at 11 pm for $20 to $40. Attractions with top billing like the magicians Siegfried & Roy, at the Mirage Casino *(Tel: (702) 792-7777)*, cost more: $80 to $90.

Stars performing are given top billing in big neon letters at casinos. It's often possible to get last-minute tickets for a show that has already had a long run. Notable longer running shows are the 'Jubilee' revues. *(Bally's Casino; Tel: (702) 739-4567)* or the 'Folies Bergères' *(Tropicana Resort; Tel: (702) 739-2414)*, 'Legends in Concert' *(Imperial Palace; Tel: (702) 794-3261)*, the 'Lance Burton Magic Show' *(Monte Carlo Casino; Tel: (702) 730-7000)* and the 'Cirque du Soleil' *(Treasure Island Casino; Tel: (702) 894-7111)*. Some casinos serve themed meals like the medieval knights' banquet 'King Arthur's Tournament' at the Excalibur or the ancient Roman symposium, the 'Bacchanal', at Caesars Palace.

INFORMATION

Las Vegas Convention & Visitors Authority
3150 S Paradise Rd.; Tel: (702) 892-7575

SURROUNDING AREA

Hoover Dam/Lake Mead   (106/B1)
★ 221 m (725 ft) high and at least 200 m (656 ft) thick at its base, the vast concrete wall of Hoover Dam restricts the flow of the Colorado River in narrow Black Canyon about 40 km (25 miles) southwest of Las Vegas. By 1922 the US government had decided to build the dam of the century to harness the raging flood waters of the Colorado. In 1935 the dam was finished after only four years of construction work. The hydroelectric power plant linked with it has 17 giant turbines, which provide Las Vegas and even part

Valley of Fire State Park: a savage contrast to the artificial casino wonderland

of southern California with electricity. The Visitor Center on the west rim of the Canyon affords spectacular views into the depths (there are 40-minute guided tours of the plant).

In the sun-scorched desert behind the dam lies Lake Mead (180 km/112 miles long), one of the world's largest man-made reservoirs. Beaches along its shores like Boulder Beach or Willow Beach are not sandy but nonetheless attractive spots for swimming. The Alan Bible Visitor Center boasts a lovely desert garden on US 93, where you can familiarize yourself with desert flora and fauna.

Red Rock Canyon   (106/A1)

The grotesque rock formations of Red Rock Canyon are only a half-hour drive west of Las Vegas. This is the perfect place for having your first sight of real Wild West scenery. A 20 km (13 mile)-long scenic highway goes to lookout points and hiking trails through the roughly 330 sq km (130 sq miles) nature preserve in the Mojave Desert *(Visitor Center at the start of the Scenic Hwy.)*. Shoot-outs are re-created daily near the entrance to the Old West town theme park, Old Nevada/Bonnie Springs.

Valley of Fire   (106/B1)

The name 'Valley of Fire' stands for distinctive rusty red sandstone rock formations about 90 km (56 miles) northeast of Las Vegas. Short trails like the one to Mouse's Tank lead into magnificent canyons carved into the rock here by over 150 million years of wind and cloudbursts. You might also enjoy combining a day trip here with an excursion to the shores of man-made Lake Mead. *Visitor Center, campground and picnic tables*

Romantic Wild West and raging waters

There are still cowboys and Indians galore in Arizona as well as fabulous golf resorts, chic galleries and trendy cafés

On car licence plates Arizona boasts of being the *Grand Canyon State* and that's not exaggerating in claiming a true wonder of the world. Yet this vast gorge in Arizona's far north is not typical of the state, which covers an area of only 300,000 sq km (116,000 sq miles). It would be more accurate to describe what makes Arizona distinctively memorable as the juxtaposition of sharp contrasts.

It's astonishing how dense coniferous forests suddenly give way to arid desert, spiky with grand Saguaro cactus like a surreal forest of telephone poles, all in the space of a few bends of the highway. One moment you'll be in what seems like the end of the world, a dusty Wild West town, expecting John Wayne to come out of a saloon any minute, and then, just a short drive away, you'll be marvelling at tinkling waterfalls in the artificially landscaped environment of a luxurious holiday resort. Even the

Natural monoliths near Sedona

climate varies wildly; crisp Christmas cold at ski resorts like Flagstaff is just as normal as shimmering, scorching heat around Phoenix and Tucson in summer. Arizona is indeed a land of contrasts and this is equally true of its blend of cultures and languages. Ancient Indian tribes still have their enclaves while modern American leisure culture is ubiquitous in shopping malls and water parks. The influence of nearby Mexico on Arizona cuisine, art and architecture is unmistakable since immigrants cross the border daily, both legally and illegally.

Only 150 years ago Arizona was the wildest part of the Wild West. Renegade gunslingers made life dangerous in mining towns. Apaches and Navajos were still ambushing settlers until the US Cavalry finally subdued them in fierce battles and banished them to reservations. Yet the tribes have survived to become today's most rapidly growing ethnic group. The Navajo's reservation is in northeast Arizona and the Navajo is the most populous tribe in the US.

39

Superlatives are often heard in Arizona, where vast dimensions are the norm. This is where America's biggest man-made reservoirs, Lake Mead and Lake Powell, are found. These reservoirs provide water and electricity for the state's mushrooming cities. But unfortunately the dams and reservoirs are threatening the ecosystems along the Colorado River. Once again the contrasts are extreme – in this case in politics and environmental policy.

Travelling in Arizona entails many, many hours spent on the highways, where you'll be absorbing desert, cacti and Route 66 nostalgia. Sunsets spent around juniper-scented campfires at dude ranches, then swimming in artificial indoor lagoons at resort hotels in Scottsdale, followed by breathtaking views of the earth's history and often amazingly welcoming encounters with friendly, hospitable people. And you can be sure the next suprise is just around the next bend in the road.

BISBEE

(107/E6) This little Wild West town in the mountains of southern Arizona has retained a way of life familiar to the copper miners of 100 years ago. No new building disturbs its romantic appearance. A clutch of streets in a narrow valley is lined with everything a good Western film set needs: a bank, some saloons and a jail. For about 20 years artists and people looking for the good life have been settling in town, preserving it from decline. The history of the town and

mining is told in the little *Bisbee Mining and Historical Museum* on Copper Queen Plaza *(daily 10 am–4 pm; Admission: $3)* in great detail. The *Queen Mine* next to the vast open-face mine, *Lavender Pit*, can be inspected via a guided tour of the pit.

High Desert Inn
An upbeat dining venue housed in a former prison. Imaginative seafood and poultry dishes. *8 Naco Rd.; Tel: (520) 432-1442; Category 2–3*

Copper Queen
Once an elegant hotel catering for mining tycoons and now tastefully restored in period style with restaurant and saloon. *46 rooms; 11 Howell Ave.; Tel: (520) 432-2216; Fax: 432-4298; Category 2*

Schoolhouse Inn
A delightful B & B with accommodation in the classrooms of an old schoolhouse. *9 rooms; 818 Tombstone Canyon St.; Tel and Fax: (520) 432-2996; Category 3*

CANYON DE CHELLY NATIONAL MONUMENT

(107/F1-2) ★ These two spectacular gorges on what is now a Navajo reservation afforded the Anasazi a safe refuge and, in the canyon bottoms, arable land for agriculture 800 years ago when their sophisticated civilisation was flourishing. The Anasazi cliff

MARCO POLO SELECTION: ARIZONA

1 Arizona-Sonora Desert Museum
An outstanding desert museum (page 52)

2 The Borgata
Elegant shopping in a replica of San Gimignano (page 48)

3 Canyon de Chelly National Monument
Wild canyons on a Navajo reservation (pages 40–41)

4 San Xavier del Bac Mission
A 'white dove in the desert': Arizona's finest Mission church (page 52)

5 The Museum Club
A Route 66 venue for Harley fans and the young at heart (page 42)

6 Schnebly Hill Road
Red rocks and scenery straight out of a Western (page 49)

dwellings of worked stone are clearly discernible on the walls of one 50 km (31 mile) long and 300 m (984 ft)-deep canyon. The most ✈ magnificent views to be had from North Rim Drive (best light: before noon) from the *Mummy Cave Overlook* and the *Antelope House Overlook.* In the late afternoon the *White House Overlook* (with a trail down into the canyon) and the *Spider Rock Overlook* on South Rim Drive are at their best.

SIGHTS

Navajo guides take visitors into the canyons, where Navajo families still live, by four-wheel-drive vehicle or on horseback. Info: *Thunderbird Lodge (Tel: (520) 674-5841)* and *Justin's Horse Rental (Tel: (520) 674-5678).*

HOTEL

Holiday Inn Canyon de Chelly
A new complex in the adobe style near the Park entrance. Pool, 108 rooms, a small restaurant. *P.O. Box 1889, Chinle; Tel: (520) 674-5000; Fax: 674-8264; Category 2*

SURROUNDING AREA

Hopi Reservation   (107/E1-2)
About 3,000 years ago the ancestors of the Hopi settled the three mesas in what is now a reservation, building villages like *Walpi* and *Oraibi* on the cliffs. Strongly tradition-minded, the Hopi cling to their ancient ceremonies and segregate themselves from the white man. Even taking pictures is strictly forbidden on the reservation. The *Hopi Cultural Center* on Second Mesa gives a good idea of how the tribe lives. There you can find out exactly when seasonal Navajo ceremonial dancing is to take place.

Hubbell Trading Post   (107/E2)
This picturesque trading post dating from 1878 is now a protected historic monument. Exhibitions in the Visitor Center and demonstrations of Native Amer-

ican weaving. *Near Ganado on Hwy. 264*

FLAGSTAFF

(107/D2) The first impression of northern Arizona's biggest city (pop. 46,000) sprawled along Route 66 is not all that exciting. However, Flagstaff boasts numerous excellent motels, which makes it the perfect starting point for tours to the Grand Canyon (always booked out) and Sedona. The city itself and its environs are worth a stay. A lively student scene keeps the meticulously restored old town, which is easy to explore on foot, hopping. Moreover, you should take the time to visit the remarkable *Lowell Observatory (1400 Mars Hill Rd.),* where the planet Pluto was discovered in 1930, and superb *Walnut Canyon* at the eastern end of town, where the Sinagua Indians settled 800 years ago (the trail to the ruins is labelled). Just north of Flagstaff the once volcanic peaks of the San Francisco Mountains are ideal territory to explore on foot and by mountain bike.

MUSEUM

Museum of Northern Arizona
Excellent exhibitions dealing with natural history and Native American cultures around the Grand Canyon. *Daily 9 am–5 pm; Admission: $5; Fort Valley Rd.; 5 km (3 miles) to the north on US 180; Tel: (520) 774-5213*

RESTAURANTS

Flagstaff Brewing Company
❧ A lively venue in the old town with a long bar, pleasant patio and live music every evening. *16 E Route 66; Tel: (520) 773-1442; Category 3*

Pasto
Italian-inspired cuisine in an elegant old-town ambience. *19 E Aspen St.; Tel: (520) 779-1937; Category 2–3*

HOTELS

Flagstaff La Quinta Inn
Although right at the intersection of three highways, in a peaceful wooded location. Modern, 3 km (2 miles) from old town. *122 rooms; 2355 S Beulah Blvd.; Tel: (520) 556-8666; Fax: 214-9140; Category 2–3*

Monte Vista
Romantic old-town ambience behind an old brick façade at the centre of town. *65 rooms; 100 N San Francisco St.; Tel: (520) 779-6971; Fax: 779-2904; Category 2–3*

ENTERTAINMENT

The Museum Club
★ A big old log cabin right on Route 66 with an imaginatively decorated interior and great Country music till 1 am. *3404 E Route 66*

INFORMATION

Flagstaff Visitors Bureau
Info Center in the historic old-town train station. Tel: (520) 774-9541; Fax: 556-1305

SURROUNDING AREA

Sunset Crater
National Monument   (107/D2)
A weird lava landscape abutting the San Francisco Mountains,

crowned by an ore tip that glows red-hot in the rays of the setting sun. More than 800 years ago the Sinagua tribe used the fertile volcanic soil as arable land for agriculture. You can visit the ruins of their settlements on the circular trails through neighbouring *Wupatki National Monument,* a rewarding hike. *30 km (19 miles) to the north on Hwy. 89*

GRAND CANYON NATIONAL PARK

(107/D1) The world's biggest gorge is also the Southwest's most fabulous attraction. The rusty-red and ochre-coloured walls drop sheer to the Colorado River, 1,700 m (5,577 ft) below the rim. The Colorado carved the canyon over a period of 10 million years; it is nearly 450 km (279 miles) long and up to 30 km (19 miles) wide in places. The rock strata exposed on the walls go back 2 billion years. As breathtaking as this view of geological history is, it draws astronomical numbers of visitors each year, at least 5 million of them. Tourism on such a scale creates problems of logistics: in summer, hotel rooms on the Canyon rim are in as short supply as drinking water, which has to be brought in by tank car.

At 2,100 m (6,890 ft) above sea level, the *South Rim* is open to the public all year round. This is where you'll find the most spectacular lookout points (✧✧ Yaki Point, Mather Point), good hiking trails and the *Grand Canyon Village* with hotels, shops and museums. On ✧✧ *West Rim Drive* free shuttle buses run as far as

Hermit's Rest. A much more peaceful and less crowded spot is closed in winter: the *North Rim.* To get into the mood, you should see the Grand Canyon film in the IMAX movie theatre at Tusayan **(107/D2)** on Hwy. 180.

Hotels in the park usually have better than average to fine (✧✧ *El Tovar*) restaurants or cafeterias, as does the Desert View Lookout Point at the eastern end of East Rim Drive. In Tusayan **(107/D2)** Taco Bell, McDonalds, Denny's and Pizza Hut cater for the hungry masses.

The Steakhouse
Bustling, jam-packed, loud and busy — but the great ambience and superb steaks are worth it. *On Hwy. 180 in Tusayan across from the IMAX; Tel: (520) 638-2780; Category 2–3*

HOTELS

National Park Lodges
Hotel accommodation in the park (six hotels on the South Rim, one on the North) and rides on mules with a night at the *Phantom Ranch* on the Canyon floor should be booked as far in advance as possible.

Book reservations centrally through *Amfac Parks & Resorts, 14001 E Iliff St., Suite 600, Aurora, CO 80014; Tel: (303) 297-2757; Fax: 297-3175.*

Last-minute bookings: *Tel: (520) 638-2631.* All lodges in the Park are category 1 and 2. The town of Tusayan also has accommodation at the **(107/D2)** entrance to the park.

Quality Inn Grand Canyon

A modern inn with pleasant rooms and quiet despite its location. The restaurant is good but fairly expensive. *172 rooms; Tusayan; Tel: (520) 638-2673; Fax: 638-9537; Category 2*

Rafting

White-water rafting excursions on the Colorado lasting several days are featured by several companies (like *Grand Canyon Expeditions; Tel: (801) 644-2691).* Best to book far in advance at your travel agent's. On the spot info at the Visitor Center.

Hiking through the Canyon

To hike into the Canyon on the *South Kaibab Trail* (11 km/7 miles one way) or the *Bright Angel Trail* (15 km/9 miles) down to the banks of the Colordo River you should pick a cool day. In mid-summer the temperature in the Canyon can rise above 50°C (154°F)! Whatever you do, don't forget water! The most beautiful place for a hike that takes several days is a tributary canyon, *Havasu Canyon,* which has really magnificent waterfalls on the Havasupai Indian reservation *(Advance booking necessary; Tel: (520) 448-2141 or 448-2121).*

Flights

Even without booking in advance you can still get helicopter flights over the Canyon, for instance with *Papillon Grand Canyon Helicopters (Tel: (520) 638-2419)* or with *AirStar Helicopters (Tel: (520) 638-2622).*

Grand Canyon National Park

Large *Visitor Center* with *Museum* in Grand Canyon Village. Book in advance for overnight hikes:

Mules have right of way: descent into the Grand Canyon

Backcountry Office, P.O. Box 129, Grand Canyon, AZ 86023; Tel: (520) 638-7888

KINGMAN

(106/B2) This rather dreary desert town in northwestern Arizona is usually just a stop for truckers and tourists between Flagstaff and Las Vegas. However, Kingman is located on the legendary Route 66 and is immortalized in Bobby Trump's 1950s song. The best memorabilia for fans are in the restaurant called *Mr. D'z (105 E Andy Devine Ave.)* and the lobby, packed with Route 66 memorabilia, of the *Quality Inn (1400 E Andy Devine Ave.)*.

SURROUNDING AREA

Route 66   **(106/B-C2)**
Highway fans and Harley freaks gravitate towards the stretch of the old original road: via *Hackberry* (a wonderfully crazy Visitor's Center for Route 66) and *Peach Springs* to *Grand Canyon Caverns* (a traditional Route 66 place to make a break). Just a handful of houses in a hilly no man's land with rusty neon signs dangling from long since derelict motels: *Bonjour, tristesse!*

LAKE POWELL/PAGE

(101/D6) Upriver from the Grand Canyon the 216 m (825 ft)-high *Glen Canyon Dam* near Page, built in 1964, has harnessed the Colorado River in a vast reservoir, the second largest in the USA. A labyrinth of bays, grotesque rocky islets and red canyons with over 3,000 km (1,860 miles) of shoreline, this is a para-dise for water sports enthusiasts. The little town of *Page* on the southern rim of the dam has mushroomed from a camp for the labourers who built the dam to a popular starting point for boat trips. You mustn't miss the exhibitions in the *Carl Hayden Visitor's Center* on the northern edge of the dam, where visitors can descend into the vast caverns that contain the generator.

HOTELS

Best Western Arizona Inn
A good motel on the outskirts of town, lovely views *(ask for a room with a lake view). 103 rooms; 716 Rim View Dr.; Tel: (520) 645-2466; Fax: 645-2053; Category 2–3*

Wahweap Lodge
A modern hotel village with 350 rooms. Perhaps a bit impersonal but nevertheless right on the lake. *100 Lakeshore Dr.; Tel: (520) 645-2433; Fax: 645-1031; Category 2*

SPORTS & LEISURE

Boat and raft trips and *fully furnished houseboats* for longer trips on the lake must be booked well in advance *(Tel: (602) 278-8888; Fax: 331-5258;* last-minute bookings: *Tel: (520) 645-2433). Guided hikes* to the breathtakingly beautiful tributary canyons like *Antelope Canyon* are arranged by the *Page Chamber of Commerce (Tel: (520) 645-2741)* for visitors.

MONUMENT VALLEY

(107/E1) Years of Westerns and television commercials have immortalized the powerful monoliths and red mesas of the desert valley right on the Utah-Arizona border. This world-famous valley is part of the Navajo reservation and Native American families still live here just as they always have in their round hogans. The best-known rock formations are the two upright sandstone *Mittens,* which seem to guard the valley. From the ☙ Visitor Center of the *Navajo Tribal Park* you can take excursions to the rock formations by jeep, minibus or on horseback, accompanied by Navajo guides. Another remarkable site to visit is the Anasazi ruins of Betatakin in the *Navajo National Monument.*

HOTELS

Goulding's Lodge
The only accommodation in the valley, a good motel with superb ☙ views. Book well in advance! *64 rooms.; P. O. Box 1, Monument Valley; Tel: (801) 727-3231; Fax: 727-3344; Category 2*

Wetherill Inn Motel
A standard-quality motel, but a good alternative if Goulding's Lodge is booked up. *54 rooms; Kayenta, Hwy. 163; Tel: (520) 697-3231; Fax: 697-3233; Category 2–3*

NOGALES

(107/E6) This is just the place for anyone who has always yearned for Mexico, for the town (pop. 20,000) is cut in two by the border. Just leave your car on the US side of the border (guarded for $3) and saunter into Mexico (you need a passport), where you'll find the *Avenida Obregón* full of colourful shops and (at the far end) nice cafés.

HOTEL

Rio Rico Resort
In a beautiful hilly setting between Nogales and Tubac, an elegant complex with pool and golf course. *175 rooms; Rio Rico, 1069 Camino Caralampi; Tel: (520) 281-1901; Fax: 281-7132; Category 1–2*

SURROUNDING AREA

Tubac **(107/D6)**
Tubac was founded in 1691, the first Spanish settlement in Arizona. Nowadays the town boasts artists' studios and art galleries as well as the magnificent ruins of the 300-year-old *Tumacacori Mission Church.*

ORGAN PIPE CACTUS NATIONAL MONUMENT

(106/C5-6) Far from civilisation on the southern border of Arizona, one of the wildest desert regions is a nature reserve. Two ☙ panaramic highways are the gateways to the Park. It is especially lovely when flowers are in bloom in April/May.

PETRIFIED FOREST NATIONAL PARK

(107/E2-3) More than 220 million years ago a prehistoric swamp swallowed up an area of huge tree trunks. Covered with layers of sediment, the hidden tree trunks slowly petrified. Erosion over hundreds of thousands of years has re-exposed them to view. Along the 46 m (150 ft)-long scenic highway through the park, you can marvel at these giant trees from nature trails, some of them shimmering in opaline tints. The *Rainbow Forest Museum (daily 8 am–5 pm)* at the north entrance is instructive on the geology of the park and the fascinating, brightly hued hills of the *Painted Desert* all around.

PHOENIX/ SCOTTSDALE

(107/D4) The proud skyline spiked with skyscrapers mirroring the heavens proclaims from afar that this is Arizona's capital and biggest city. The sprawling metropolis (pop. 2.5 million) in the broad valley of the Salt River, which is usually dried up, is fighting an unending battle against the desert climate: scorching sun and temperatures up to 40°C (104°F) keep the air-conditioning on full blast: only the fine irrigation sprays on café patios protect customers from dehydration.

The city centre doesn't offer all that much in the way of sights to see, except for the ultra-modern round *Arizona Center* (arcades, shops, cafés) and the vast saddleback roof of the *Bank One Stadium.* What makes Phoenix so attractive are its suburbs, notably Scottsdale. There you'll find Arizona's best golf courses, most elegant boutiques and most expensive luxury hotels. Be sure not to miss the studio-house called *Taliesin West (108 St./ Cactus Rd.)* where Frank Lloyd Wright lived and *Fashion Square (Scottsdale Rd./Camelback Rd.)* as well as the Wild West town of *Rawhide* to the north. Only small enclaves remain of the original desert landscape, for example *Papago Park,* where the *Phoenix Zoo* houses desert animals and the superb *Desert Botanical Garden* with more than 20,000 cacti and desert plants from all over the world.

MUSEUMS

Heard Museum

A comprehensive collection of Southwest Native American artefacts, with a fine kachina exhibition. *Daily 10 am–5 pm; Sun from 12 noon; Admission: $6; 22 E Monte Vista Rd.*

Pueblo Grande

The ruins on the banks of the Salt River attest to the people of the Hohokam culture who once lived here. *Daily 9 am–4.45 pm, Sun from 1 pm; Admission: $2; 4619 E Washington St.*

In the Marco Polo Spirit

Marco Polo was the first true world traveller. He travelled with peaceful intentions forging links between the East and the West. His aim was to discover the world, and explore different cultures and environments without changing or disrupting them. He is an excellent role model for the 20th-century traveller. Wherever we travel we should show respect for other cultures and natural environments.

RESTAURANTS

Ed Debevic's
A nostalgic diner in the 1950s style. *2102 E Highland Ave.; Tel: (602) 956-2760; Category 3*

Jean Claude's Petit Café
❖ A young, upbeat bistro serving light French cuisine. *Scottsdale; 7340 E Shoeman Lane; Tel: (602) 947-5288; Category 2–3*

Pinnacle Peak Patio
A vast steak house in the hills on the northern fringe of the city. Cowboy bands and shoot-outs liven the place up. *10426 E Jomax Rd.; Tel: (602) 585-1599; Category 2*

Top of the Rock
A high-class restaurant with ↙ scenic views in Buttes Resort, serving new Southwest cuisine. *Tempe, 2000 Westcourt Way; Tel: (602) 225-9000; Category 1–2*

SHOPPING

The place for window-shopping is *Old Scottsdale*, with all its bou-tiques and galleries along Main Street or, alternatively, browsing in any of the big malls: *Biltmore Fashion Park (Camelback Rd./24th St.)* or in a mall built in the style of an an Italian village, ★ *Borgata (6166 N Scottsdale Rd.)*. For dis-count bargains it's well worth driving to the *Arizona Factory Shops (I-17, Exit 229)* or the new *Arizona Mills (1500 W Baseline Rd.)*.

HOTELS

Embassy Suites
Unabashedly middle class with 183 spacious rooms and pool. Centrally located near the air-port, downtown and Scottsdale. *2333 E Thomas Rd.; Tel: (602) 957-1910; Fax: 955-2861; Category 2*

Royal Palms
An elegant small hotel at the foot of Camelback Mountain, with a pool and a beautiful garden. The restaurant serves superb food. *116 rooms; 5200 Camelback Rd.; Tel: (602) 840-3610; Fax: 840-6927; Category 1–2*

Scottsdale Princess
An oasis of luxury in the des-ert. Outstanding restaurants and sports facilities plus two 18-hole golf courses. *600 rooms; Scottsdale; 7575 E Princess Dr.; Tel: (602) 585-4848; Fax: 585-0086; Category 1*

ENTERTAINMENT

You'll find elegant bars and nightclubs in larger resorts. Coun-try and Western fans should drop into ❖ *Toolie's Country Saloon (4231 W Thoas Rd.)* or in the *Rockin' Horse (7000 E Indian School Rd.)*. For good rock go to

Saguaro cactus blooms in May

the *Roxy (2110 E Highland Ave.).* Dancing is great at the *Jetz/Stixx (7077 E Camelback Rd.)* or ✝ *Studebaker's (10345 N Scottsdale Blvd.).*

Phoenix Visitor's Bureau
One Arizona Center, 400 E Van Buren St., Suite 600, Phoenix, AZ 85004; Tel: (602) 252-5588; Fax: 253-4415

SURROUNDING AREA

Apache Trail   (107/D-E4)
The still partly unsurfaced Hwy. 88 winds through the country east of Phoenix with superb 🚗 views of the desert mountains. On the way to *Globe* (Wild West ambience), you will pass *Tortilla Flat,* which has a cowboy saloon; reservoirs like *Apache Lake* and *Roosevelt Lake* and beyond *Tonto National Monument* you'll be enchanted by ancient Salado cliff dwellings.

PRESCOTT

(106/C3) Despite the city being founded in 1863 as a gold-prospector camp, ranchers and loggers have still managed to leave their mark. About 100 years ago, Prescott (pop. 27,000) was actually Arizona's capital for a short period. It's a pleasant surprise to find that tourism has made virtually no impression on these quiet streets lined with authentic Western houses. The *Sharlot Hall Museum (415 W GurleySt.)* comprises several historic houses, which have been restored to make a theme park for pioneer history.

HOTEL

St. Michael
A historic downtown hotel with lots of charm and a pleasant café. *72 rooms; 205 W Gurley St.; Tel: (520) 776-1999; Fax: 776-7318; Category 3*

SEDONA

(107/D3) Almost as if modelled by an inspired sculptor, impressive red rock formations and extensive mountain forests frame this town, the home of artists and golfers (pop. 8,000). The German Surrealist painter Max Ernst, who lived here in exile during the Third Reich period, was inspired by Sedona's spectacular scenery. Nowadays its aura draws hosts of New Age adherents. The views are at their most superb from ★ *Schnebly Hill Road,* Hwy. 179 to the golfer's paradise at Oak Creek and on the way to Boynton Canyon. The attractive Hispano-Mexican style artists' colony of *Tlaquepaque* at the centre of town boasts good galleries, craftshops and places to eat.

RESTAURANTS

L'Auberge de Sedona
An outstanding gourmet restaurant in a stylishly decorated log cabin with a delightful patio on the river. *L'Auberge Lane; Tel: (520) 282-7131; Category 1*

The Heartline Café
This is the place to enjoy imaginative cuisine in an attractive artist colony atmosphere. *1610 W US 89A; Tel: (520) 282-0785; Category 2–3*

Enchantment Resort

Sporty yet elegant holiday colony in adobe style, idyllic location. *162 rooms; 525 Boynton Canyon Rd.; Tel: (520) 282-2900; Fax: 282-9249; Category 1*

Quality Inn King's Ransom

The new annex to what is otherwise an average hotel is comfortable with superb views, yet reasonably priced. *66 rooms; 771 Hwy. 79; Tel: (520) 282-7151; Fax: 282-5208; Category 2*

Chamber of Commerce

Information also on balloon trips, jeep tours and golf courses. *Info office at intersection Hwy. 89A/Forest Rd.; Tel: (520) 282-7722*

Jerome   (107/D3)

A picturesque town with lots of Wild West ambience, nestled on a mountain slope with superb ◁▷ panoramic views across the broad Verde Valley. In 1953 the last copper mine was shut down and Arizona's fifth largest city suddenly had a population of 50. Now about 500 people live here, among them many artists and gallery owners. Places of interest include: the *Gold King Museum* and saloons like the *Spirit Room* or *Paul and Jenny's.*

Oak Creek Canyon   (107/D2-3)

Hwy. 89 A runs north through the beautiful Oak Creek Valley to Flagstaff. Well worth stopping to see: *Slide Rock State Park* (natural water slide and a natural swimming pool in the rock).

TOMBSTONE

(107/E6) Main Street is dusty, the porches on old clapboard houses lean at crazy angles, the sheriff is in the saloon and people ride in red stagecoaches: that's how the Wild West really was and that's how Tombstone, Arizona has remained to this day. It may have been re-created for tourists but it's still more than just a theme park. In 1880 millions of dollars worth of gold and silver were being mined and the villains of

---

Flashfloods are no joke

On southern Arizona and New Mexico highways you'll keep seeing signs that warn: *flash floods.* What are they warning against? What do they mean by floods out in the desert? The sun is shining and there's neither a cloud in the sky nor a drop of rain in sight. Even so, these signs must be taken seriously. It's quite possible that down the road in the mountains it might be raining. That means that dried-up creek beds can suddenly become raging torrents and if you camp in *arroyos* or park your car in a low spot along the highway, you may have a surprise, a dangerous one too, because stones caught up in the floodwaters can batter your car to scrap metal. Campers have been known to have become submerged in such flashfloods.

San Xavier del Bac Mission

that era are buried in the *Boothill Cemetery,* in peaceful solitude. The famous shoot-out between Sheriff Wyatt Earp, Doc Holliday and the Clanton Gang at the *O.K. Corral* is staged every first and third Sunday at 2 pm for visitors to watch.

RESTAURANT

Big Nose Kate's Saloon
Waitresses wearing bodices and garters, cowboy music, ice-cold beer and quite good meals with lots of local colour. *Main St.; Tel: (520) 457-3405; Category 3*

HOTEL

Ironhorse Ranch
A working ranch (20,000 ha/ 49,000 acres) with imaginatively designed guest houses in the desert hills about 10 km (6 miles) out of town. *24 rooms; Kellar Rd./ Hwy. 82; P.O. Box 536; Tel: (520) 457-9361; Fax: 457-2471; meals and horseback riding; Category 1*

TUCSON

(**107/D-E5**) Visitors to Tucson expecting to find a rough, trigger-happy environment straight from a typical Western will be utterly amazed on arriving here. This is a pleasantly air-conditioned city (pop. 850,000) set in the broad, cactus-studded desert valley of southern Arizona. A large university, the computer industry and aviation provide jobs; golf courses and fabulous resort hotels are inducements to stay.

The healthy, dry climate (sunshine 350 days a year) of the Sonora Desert is what has made the city grow by leaps and bounds since World War II. Winters in Tucson are agreeably mild; although summers here are hot, days spent lazing by the pool more than make up for the blistering heat. Don't fail to do some sightseeing: in the charmingly restored Old-Town, *El Presidio,* the lively student quarter around 4th Avenue and the *cactus forests* all around.

SIGHTS

Old Tucson Studios
After a fire in 1995, the famous sets, where so many popular Westerns have been filmed, has opened its doors again. There are stunt shows daily. *In winter daily 9 am–6 pm, in summer 9 am–9 pm; Admission: $14.95; in Tucson Mountain Park*

Saguaro National Park
Set in the hills both east and west of Tucson, this park has two sections: a nature reserve where ancient Saguaro cacti up to 15 m (49 ft) high (bloom time in May) are

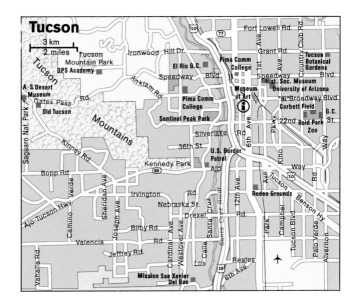

Tucson

3 km
2 miles

Tucson Mountain Park
DPS Academy
Ironwood Hill Dr.
El Rio G.C.
Pima Comm College
Tucson Botanical Gardens
Speedway Blvd
A.-S. Desert Museum
Gates Pass Rd.
Old Tucson
Anklam Rd.
Pima Comm College
Museum of Art
Hist. Soc. Museum
University of Arizona
Hi-Broadway Blvd
Corbett Field
Sentinel Peak Park
Silverlake Rd.
22nd Reid Park St.
Zoo
Saguaro Nat. Park
Kinney Rd.
36th St.
U.S. Border Patrol
Kennedy Park
Ajo
Bopp Rd.
Irvington Rd
Nebraska St
Rodeo Grounds
Sheridan Ave
Joseph Ave
Camino Verde
Ajo-Tucson Hwy
Bilby Rd.
Drexel Rd.
Valencia
Cardinal Ave
Westover Ave
Calle Santa Cruz
Park
Campbell
Tucson Blvd
Patio Verde
Alvernon
Jeffrey Rd.
Los
Reales
6th Ave
Mission San Xavier Del Bac

protected. Labelled Nature Trails and roads start from Visitor Centers, taking you through this unspoilt desert scenery. *Daily 8 am–5 pm*

San Xavier del Bac Mission

★ In 1700, Father Eusebio Kino founded the first Spanish mission station in the Tohono O'odham tribal territory. The present church dates from 1797. Superb murals on the walls. *Daily 8 am–6 pm; Admission free; 15 km/9 miles to the south on San Xavier Rd.*

MUSEUMS

Arizona-Sonora Desert Museum

★ The living desert: nowhere is it better presented than in this theme park, with American desert flora and fauna. *Daily 7.30 am–6 pm, in winter 8.30 am–5 pm; Admission: $8.95; in Tucson Mountain Park*

Arizona State Museum

An outstanding ethnographic collection of Native American artefacts from the Southwest. *Mon–Sat 10 am–5 pm, Sun from 12 noon; Admission free; Park Ave./ University Blvd.*

Pima Air and Space Museum

Over 200 old airplanes sleep peacefully in the dry desert, surrounded by an airplane graveyard, where thousands of old bombers have been retired. *Daily 9 am–5 pm; Admission: $6; 6000 E Valencia Rd.*

RESTAURANTS

Café Terra Cotta

A stylish place with patio, on St Philip's Plaza. Imaginative, and superlative, Southwest cuisine. *4280 N Campbell Ave.; Tel: (520) 577-8100; Category 1–2*

Li'l Abner's Steakhouse

The house speciality is big, succulent charcoal-grilled steaks, served where Wild West stagecoaches really stopped. *8500 N Silverbell Rd.; Tel: (520) 744-2800; Category 2*

HOTELS

Omni Tucson National

Ideal for golf with all the comforts of a posh desert resort. Spacious, elegant casitas, three 9-hole golf courses. *140 rooms; 2727 W Club Dr.; Tel: (520) 297-2271; Fax: 742-2452; Category 1*

La Posada del Valley

Attractive B & B in an historic adobe house with a garden. *5 rooms; 1640 N Campbell Ave.; Tel and Fax: (520) 795-3840; Category 2–3*

Westward Look Resort

A spacious holiday complex with lovely ☁️ views across the desert. Tennis, 3 pools, good restaurant. *244 rooms; 245 W Ina Rd.; Tel: (520) 297-1151; Fax: 297-9023; Category 2*

ENTERTAINMENT

What you'll want to listen to in Tucson is Country and Western, at ❖ *Cactus Moon Café (5470 E Broadway Blvd.)* or in a big Western saloon like *The New West (4385 W Ina Rd.).* If you prefer to listen to some jazz and blues, then try the *Chicago Bar (5954 E Speedway Blvd.).* Watch students guzzling at ☀ *Club Congress (311 E Congress St.)* or listening to rock 'n' roll at *Outback (296 N Stone Ave.).*

INFORMATION

Tucson Convention & Visitors Bureau

130 S Scott Ave., Tucson, AZ 85701; Tel: (520) 624-1817; Fax: 884-7804

SURROUNDING AREA

Biosphere 2 (107/E5)

Near Oracle, an hour's drive north of Tucson, life in the future is being tested. The bizarre glass pyramids house the initially controversial project that was financed by the Texas millionaire Hunts. Researchers lived here from 1991 to 1993, studying life in an artificial environment. Futher research is now being conducted by scientists from world-famous Columbia University (guided tours).

Biosphere 2, an eerie experiment in living in the future

The land of red rock

*Dramatic natural arches and fiery red canyons —
nature is at her grandest
in the Mormon state of Utah*

Utah boasts even more natural wonders than the far more famous state of Arizona with its Grand Canyon. Most of the Colorado Plateau lies to the north of the Grand Canyon. On this part of the Colorado Plateau, sandstone and limestone formations between 200 and 300 million years old have been hewn by rivers, wind and weather into dramatic gorges with steep walls and natural rock sculpture. Southern Utah alone has five national parks, as well as numerous national monuments, state parks and other nature reserves, ranging from the filigree rock columns of Bryce Canyon to the stone wonderland of Canyonlands and Arches National Parks. Nowhere else on earth are so many natural wonders at such close quarters.

However, Utah is not just red, rocky desert. In the north of the state (surface area approx 220,000 sq km/137,500 sq miles)

*Bryce Canyon National Park:
iron and manganese colour the rock*

deserts stretch around the shores of the Great Salt Lake, formed during the last American Ice Age, as far as the Wasatch Mountains, outliers of the Rockies, where green valleys and mountain trails await hikers and mountain bikers. In winter the region is one of the world's best places to ski. Top skiers from across the world will meet here in the year 2002 because its legendary powder snow and superb terrain have made it the designated venue for the 2002 Winter Olympics.

Despite ultra-modern lift infrastructure, excellent highways and a growing high-tech economy in cities like Salt Lake City and Provo, Utah has remained pioneer country to this day. It is still very thinly populated: only about 2 million people live in this vast area. Most of the population is concentrated in greater Salt Lake City. This has always been sparsely settled country. Even the Ute tribe, who have given the state its name, once roamed the vast region in small family groups as hunters and gatherers. Trappers and early settlers tended to avoid this impressive but arid and forbidding rocky country.

The Mormons were the first to settle permanently in the desert around the Great Salt Lake. After the historic trek known as the Mormon Trail, they arrived here to proclaim a theocracy and to make the desert arable land through irrigation. Even today most residents of Utah are Mormon descendants. Although Utah is a normal federal state, politics here often bear the stamp of Mormon principles. Alcohol, for instance, is sold only in public stores, served only in restaurants with meals or at the bars of clubs where membership is compulsory. Beer is all that's available in saloons and small bars.

If at all possible, take your time to marvel at the magnificent and breathtaking scenery; get on the trail and enjoy the unspoilt nature that abounds in the state of Utah.

BLUFF/BLANDING

(**101/E6**) These historic pioneer towns in southeastern Utah are a good place to start from if you want to explore the interior, where canyons in *Natural Bridges National Monument* and Native American ruins in *Edge of the Cedars State Park* (museum) await you. Moreover, the tributary canyons of *Lake Powell* are accessible from here. If you go further afield, you might enjoy a round trip through the *Valley of the Gods* with its dramatic rock towers and to *Muley Point Overlook* on the San Juan River, a must!

BOULDER

(**101/D6**) Boulder is just a tiny ranching town on Hwy. 12, yet the magnificent canyons, most of them pristine wilderness, around it bear comparision with any national park. This is a marvellous place for getting out into the wilds on foot, by jeep or on horseback. In autumn 1996,

MARCO POLO SELECTION: UTAH

1 Antelope Island
Read the paper while floating on Salt Lake
(page 65)

2 Boulder Mountain Lodge
For adventure holidays: a lodge in canyon country
(page 57)

3 Bryce Canyon
A wonderland of filigree sandstone columns
(page 57)

4 Dead Horse Point
The best views across the canyons
(page 61)

5 Delicate Arch
The classic postcard motif: a free-standing fiery red natural arch
(page 61)

6 Zion Narrows
Superlative wilderness backpacking (page 67)

President Clinton designated the region between Boulder and Escalante in the *Escalante-Grand Staircase National Monument* as a nature reserve. By taking the only partly paved ◁▷ *Burr Trail,* a historic pioneer route, you can drive deep into the vast, stony heart of Capitol Reef National Park.

Boulder Mountain Lodge

★ A modern, cosy lodge with only 20 guest rooms. Ideal starting point for trips in four-wheel-drive vehicles, for backpacking or exploring the region on horseback. *On Hwy. 12; Tel: (435) 335-7460; Fax: 335-7461; Category 2–3*

BRYCE CANYON NATIONAL PARK

(101/D5-6) ★ After the Grand Canyon, this small national park (covering an area of only 146 sq km/90 sq miles) is the most beautiful and popular in the Southwest. It's a wonderland of red and white rock columns, deeply fissured rock walls and stony natural castles. Rain and winter frosts over millions of years have formed these grotesque rock sculptures from the brightly coloured sandstone on the steep escarpment of Paunsaugunt Plateau. Incidentally, the nature reserve, established in 1928, was named after Ebenezer Bryce, a Mormon settler. Before that, the Paiute tribe called this valley of natural wonders 'Unkatimpewa-wince-pock-ich' which, roughly translated, means 'red rocks like standing men in a

Riding in Bryce Canyon

valley', really a very succinct and apt description.

From the *Visitor Center* (exhibitions, slide show), about 30 km (19 miles) of panoramic highway follow the rim of the canyon south; short side roads feed into the most spectacular of all ◁▷ lookout points: *Fairyland Point, Bryce Point, Sunrise* and *Sunset Point* and *Rainbow Point* in the far south of the park. Magnificently beautiful and very popular for day-hikes are the trails in *Bryce Amphitheater,* though you'll find less frequented trails further south. By the way, it can get very cold in the canyon, for the rim is at an elevation of 2,400–2,700 m (7,920–8,900ft).

Accommodation at the entrance to the park is always booked up in

Adventure far from the highway

In the southern Utah canyon country and in the western Colorado mountains, you should take the time to go into the almost deserted interior. You can do this by hiking for quite some distance or by hiring a four-wheel-drive vehicle (in Moab, Grand Junction or Telluride). There are trails galore: old mining trails used by gold and uranium prospectors lead deep into the red canyons and across the high San Juan Mountain pass into Colorado. Outside national parks camping is permitted anywhere, although in the parks you need a *backcountry permit*, which is issued by park Rangers. Be sure to buy topographical maps wherever you are. Four-wheel-drive vehicle rental firms usually also have good maps and reliable tips on where you can find old mines, beautiful roads through passes, pictographs and ruins of Native American settlements.

peak season. Alternatives to staying this close are good motels and B & B inns in nearby towns like *Tropic* and the romantically authentic Mormon Western town of *Panguitch.*

Bryce Canyon Lodge

Historic hotel (1923) with log cabins, in the park near the rim of the canyon. Restaurant. *114 rooms; book as early as possible with Amfac Parks & Resorts, 14001 E Iliff St., Suite 600, Aurora, CO 80014; Tel: (303) 297-2757; Fax: 297-3175; Category 2*

Foster Family Motel

A comfortable motel with lots of personal attention to your wants; good steak restaurant. *40 rooms; on Hwy. 12 near the park entrance; Tel: (435) 834-5227; Fax: 834-5304; Category 3*

Marianna Inn Motel

A quaint little motel half an hour's drive from the park. *24 rooms; Panguitch, 669 N Main St.; Tel: (435) 676-8844; Fax: 676-8340; Category 2–3*

SPORTS & LEISURE

Bryce-Zion Trail Rides

Two to four-hour rides on horseback into the rock labyrinth. Also rides into Zion National Park. *Office in Bryce Canyon Lodge; Tel: (435) 834-5219*

INFORMATION

Bryce Canyon National Park

Bryce Canyon, UT 84717; Tel: (435) 834-5322

CAPITOL REEF NATIONAL PARK

(101/D5) Only one paved road runs through this park (area 1,000 sq km/625 sq miles), which encircles the 160 km (100 mile)-long *Waterpocket Fold.* These sandstone and limestone mountains were moulded by erosion into fantastically fissured canyons and grotesque wonderland palaces of rock. A 40 km (25 mile)-long *scenic drive* runs from the Visitor Center (lovely campsite) on Hwy. 24 into the narrow canyon called ◁▷ *Capitol Gorge.* Other, no less spectacular, parts of this park like, for instance, ◁▷ *Cathedral Valley,* are accessible by four-wheel-drive vehicles (tracks). Day trips into the interior arranged at *Torrey* on the western edge of the park.

RESTAURANT

Capitol Reef Inn & Café
A little motel with a good bookshop and a café that serves excellent country food: steaks, trout etc; *10 rooms; Torrey, 360 W Main St.; Tel: (435) 425-3271*

HOTELS

Best Western Capitol Reef Resort
Big, modern motel on the western edge of the park. Restaurant. *50 rooms; Torrey, Hwy. 24; Tel: (435) 425-3761; Fax: 425-3300; Category 2-3*

Cactus Hill Motel
A small, family-run motel in a quiet location in a historic Mormon town. *6 rooms; Teasdale, 830 South 1000 East; Tel: (435) 425-3578; no fax; Category 3*

SURROUNDING AREA

Goblin Valley   (101/E5)
Northeast of Hanksville on Hwy. 24 is a tiny gem in the midst of this canyon country: a fairy-tale valley with hundreds of little rock sculptures that look like dwarfs and mythical beasts (a lovely camp site).

CEDAR CITY

(100/C5) A Mormon town (pop. 14,000) far away from it all but

Utah's culture capital. Every summer several theatres on the Southern Utah University campus produce the Utah Shakespearean Festival with performances of Shakespeare plays that are acclaimed throughout the country. Works by other dramatists are also staged *(to book tickets: Tel: (435) 586-7878).*

SURROUNDING AREA

Cedar Breaks
National Monument   (100/C5)
One of the canyon country's smaller nature preserves is east of Cedar City on Hwy. 14: a steep escarpment with variegated limestone columns. Be sure not to miss the short trail to a stand of *Bristlecone Pines,* a species of pine that thrives here at an elevation of 3,000 m (9,800 ft), reaching an age of 4,000 years.

MOAB

(101/E5) In recent years, this small town (pop. 4,000) on a broad river terrace on the upper reaches of the Colorado has become a venue for adventure holidays and a mecca for nature lovers. It is surrounded by some of the Southwest's most beautiful nature reserves and wildest rocky country, including the famous Arches and Canyonlands National parks. Each year sees more visitors who want to experience this matchless natural beauty, exploring the region on foot, by jeep safari or white-water rafting. Numerous tour operators and sporting goods rental firms in the area feature tours and provide the equipment. Moab is especially popular with mountain bikers because their bike's tyres get good traction on the sandstone rocks when exploring the terrain. Experience it from the ⚕ Slick Rock Trail above town, where the world's best bikers meet to challenge each other's skills in competitions.

RESTAURANTS

Buck's Grill House
The latest 'in' place to eat: superb Southwest cuisine and, of course, mouth-watering steaks. *1393 Hwy. 191 N; Tel: (435) 259-5201; Category 2*

Grand Old Ranchhouse
Good American home cooking in a cosy old house. *1266 Hwy. 191 N; Tel: (435) 259-5753; Category 2–3*

Moab Brewery
⚕ A great place to quench your thirst: a brewery (top-fermented beer!) outlet. Biker venue with pizza, steak and grilled chicken. *686 S Main St.; southern fringe of town; Category 3*

Slick Rock Café
⚕ Popular with young people, Santa Fe decor and cuisine. *Center St./Main St.; Tel: (435) 259-8004; Category 2–3*

HOTELS

Best Western Canyonlands Inn
Pleasant motel owned by a chain, right in town, quiet rooms at the back. *77 rooms; 16 S Main St.; Tel: (435) 259-2300; Fax: 259-2301; Category 2*

Blue Heron B & B
A lovely place for nature lovers outside town, right in a beautiful nature reserve. *6 rooms; 900 W Kane Creek Blvd.; Tel. and Fax: (435) 259-4921; Category 2–3*

Canyon Country B & B
A cosy place with a great library. *6 rooms; 590 North 500 West; Tel: (435) 259-5262; Fax: 259-6684; Category 3*

Comfort Suites
A modern motel with indoor pool. All 75 rooms are suites. *800 S Main St.; Tel: (435) 259-5252; Fax: 259-7110; Category 2*

Sunflower Hill B & B
Rather pricey for a B & B but in a beautiful location and with all the amenities, including a whirlpool. *11 rooms; 185 North 300 East; Tel: (435) 259-2974 Fax: 259-2470; Category 2*

SPORTS & LEISURE

Adrift Adventures
Rafting and four-wheel-drive tours around Moab. *378 N Main St.; Tel: (435) 259-8594; Fax: 259-7628*

Moki Treks
Guided one-day hikes to petroglyphs and canyons around Moab. *CVSR Box 2902; Tel: (435) 259-4137; Fax: 259-2617*

Nichols Expeditions
⚕ Long hikes and mountain-bike tours into the mountains and the national parks of southeastern Utah. *497 N Main St.; Tel: (435) 259-3999; Fax: 259-2312*

Tag-a-Long Expeditions
One-day and longer four-wheel-drive and rafting tours into the interior. *452 N Main St.; Tel: (435) 259-8946; Fax: 259-8990*

Thrifty Car Rental
Four-wheel-drive vehicles for hire. *711 S Main St.; Tel: (435) 259-7317; Fax: 259-4524*

Moab Information Center
Center St./Main St., P.O. Box 550, Moab; UT 84532; Tel: (435) 259-8825; Fax: 259-1376

SURROUNDING AREA

Arches National Park   (101/E4)
This spectacular park is only 10 km (6 miles) north of Moab: a plateau high above the Colorado River, where the whipping desert winds have cut several hundred natural arches into the fiery red, roughly 150 million-year-old sandstone. A layer of salt, which high pressure turns into a tough paste, is responsible for the creation of these natural wonders. A road about 30 km (19 miles) long runs from the Visitor Center to the arches of the *Windows* section and on to the *Devils Garden* (beautiful campgrounds). From there a trail leads to some of the park's biggest natural arches. Don't miss hiking to ★ *Delicate Arch* – at its best in the late afternoon.

Canyonlands National Park   (101/E5)
The wilderness within this nature reserve (1,365 sq km/853 sq miles) southwest of Moab boasts spectacular labyrinthine gorges. The following lookout points afford the most beautiful views across this stony country: ◁▷ *Island in the Sky* high above the confluence of the Green and Colorado Rivers (accessible via Hwy. 313).

Hundreds of kilometres of track for four-wheel-drive vehicles, such as *White Rim Trail* lead deep into the canyon. *Newspaper Rock,* with its remarkable pictographs, is located in *Needles,* where there are more tracks suitable for Jeeps.

Dead Horse Point State Park   (101/E5)
★ From a narrow rock outcropping at the end of SR 313 high above the Colorado River (elevation 600 m/2,000 ft), your gaze sweeps across steep canyon walls, remote plateaus and the meanders of the river *(Visitor Center, campgrounds).*

Monument Valley   (101/E6)
Renowned from films, the valley of the red monoliths marking the southern border of Utah can be reached from *Kayenta,* a good starting-point (page 45).

Arches National Park: Double Arch

OGDEN

(**101/D2**) The railroad has left its stamp on northern Utah's biggest city (pop. 64,000) more noticeably than elsewhere: the huge shunting station has been one of the West's major rail junctions for over 100 years. The Western façades in the old saloon section on 25th Street, now a highly popular ✪ shopping street, bear witness to the early pioneer days. Ogden Valley is today one of the state's most important fruit-growing regions. Regional farm produce is for sale on roadside stands along Hwy. 89 north of the city.

MUSEUM

Union Station Museum
A large-scale model records the building of the Union Pacific Railway. Also notable: old cars, rifles and other relevant memorabilia of the Old West. *Mon–Sat 10 am–5 pm; Admission: $2; 25th St./Wall Ave.*

HOTEL

Radisson Suite
Renovated historic hotel at the centre of town. Restaurant at the top with panoramic views. *144 suites; 2510 Washington Blvd.; Tel; (801) 627-1900; Fax: 393-1258; Category 2*

SURROUNDING AREA

Golden Spike
National Historic Site (**100/C2**)
In 1869 the Transcontinental Railroad ended in the desert around the Great Salt Lake at *Promontory Point* (about an hour's

drive northwest of Ogden); it was finished off with a golden spike. After that, the settling of the West could begin in earnest. A *Visitor Center* is informative (films and exhibitions) on how the railroad was built. On 10 May and at the *Railroader's Festival* in mid-August, steam engines recreate the event.

PARK CITY

(**101/D2**) An attractively restored early silver-mining town about an hour's drive east of Salt Lake City, Park City is, together with two ski areas nearby, *Deer Valley* and *Park West,* undisputedly Utah's largest and most diverse winter sports area. Clouds from the Pacific cross more than 500 km (312 miles) of Nevada desert to unload fine, dusty-dry powder snow on the Wasatch Mountains: at least 12 m (40 ft) of it a winter. This makes for ideal skiing conditions, which is why the US ski team trains here — certainly excellent advertising for the quality of the slopes. In the year 2002 this will be the Winter Olympics venue. The giant ski jump is already in place. If you feel up to it, you can take a crash course, which includes a test jump from the Olympic ski jump.

SALT LAKE CITY

(**101/D2**) Utah's sprawling capital (pop. of Greater Salt Lake City: 1.2 million) is situated in the valley floor on the eastern edge of the Great Salt Lake against the backdrop of the Wasatch Mountains (3,500 m/11,550 ft). Despite the growth of modern industries — electronics, textile processing, utilities and energy technologies – Salt Lake City is chiefly known for being the religious centre of the Church of Jesus Christ of Latter-Day Saints, the Mormons. Many non-Mormons live in this growing city, yet the Church still shapes urban policies. Strictly enforced observance of Sunday as a day of rest and sparkling clean downtown streets attest to Mormon influence. Family values and conservative politics are the order of the day here.

Founded in 1847, Salt Lake City marked the end of the Mormon Trail for pioneers persecuted in Illinois and further east. They were able to found their theocracy in the Salt Lake depression. Many monuments in the inner city, which is laid out in a grid, commemorate the pioneer days. The city boasts attractions of a different type in winter. Utah's best ski areas, like *Alta, Snowbird* and *Park City,* are only a half hour's drive from downtown Salt Lake City.

SIGHTS

LDS Church Office Building
Lookout platform on the 26th floor of the Church administration with ☊ lovely views of the city. *Mon–Fri 9 am–4.30 pm; Admission free; 50 E North Temple St.*

Temple Square
Most of the attractions that the world centre of the Mormon

Witness in stone to enduring faith: the Salt Lake City Mormon Temple

faith has to offer centre around this square at the heart of the city. The vast temple (built between 1853 and 1893) is not open to the public, that is, to non-Mormons, although quite a few other historic buildings may be visited: the famous *Tabernacle* concert hall with one of the world's largest organs (choral performances Sun 9.30 am, Thurs 8 pm; organ concerts Mon–Sat noon, Sun 2 pm), the house of *Brigham Young,* the legendary Mormon leader, and the superbly restored ☜ *Joseph Smith Memorial Building* (guided tours, free of charge: daily 8 am–10 pm, in winter 9 am–9 pm).

This Is the Place State Park

The museum village, *Old Desert Village,* a large monument and exhibitions are informative on the pioneer trek westward. *In summer daily 10 am–6 pm; museum village 12–5pm; Admission: $5; Emigration Canyon*

Utah State Capitol

The impressive, domed state legislature was built on a hill above the inner city in 1916. It is one of America's finest. Historical exhibitions are mounted in the Capitol basement. *Mon–Fri 9 am–5 pm; guided tours Tues–Thurs*

Museum of Church History and Art

The ecclesiastical art may not be to everyone's taste but the exhibitions dealing with the Mormon faith are remarkable. Dioramas on pioneer history and the settling of the West. *Mon–Fri 9 am–9 pm, Sun 10 am–7 pm; Admission free; 45 N West Temple*

Barking Frog Grille

Stylishly trendy eatery with imaginative Southwest cuisine, in summer also on the patio. *39 W Market St.; Tel: (801) 322-3764; Category 2*

Lamb's

Utah's oldest restaurant (1919) serves hearty Mormon fare. *Sun closed; 169 S Main St.; Tel: (801) 364-7166; Category 2–3*

New Yorker

❂ Popular, trendy eatery serving seafood, pasta and salads. *60 Market St.; Tel: (801) 363-0166; Category 2*

Red Iguana

Austere furnishings but excellent Mexican cuisine. *736 W North Temple; Tel: (801) 322-1489; Category 3*

Trolley Square

❂ A large, attractively designed shopping centre in halls that once housed the city trams. Plenty of restaurants and cinemas make this a magnet for window-shopping. *600 South 700 East*

ZCMI Center

The West's oldest department store, right across from Temple Square, is still today a chic place to shop.

Anton Boxrud B & B

A lovely guest house (breakfast served) in a historic house near

the city centre. *7 rooms; 57 South
600 East; Tel: (801) 363-8035;
Fax: 596-1316; Category 2–3*

Peery
Lovingly restored old hotel in
the city centre. Good restaurant.
*77 rooms; 110 West 300 South; Tel:
(801) 521-4300; Fax: 575-5014;
Category 2–3*

Residence Inn
Modern hotel with suites near
Trolley Square on the southern
fringe of the city centre. *128
rooms; 765 East 400 South; Tel:
(801) 532-5511; Fax: 531-0416;
Category 2*

ENTERTAINMENT

The city's microbreweries have
been popular for some years
now, firms like *Red Rock Brewing
Company (254 South 200 West),*
the *Squatters Brew Pub (147 West
Broadway)* and *Fuggles (375 West
200 South).* The beer brewed here
(there's even top-brewed, German
style) tastes really good.

INFORMATION

Salt Lake
Convention & Visitors Bureau
*90 S West Temple, Salt Lake City,
UT 84101-1406; Tel: (801) 521-
2822; Fax: 534-49 27*

SURROUNDING AREA

Bingham Canyon   (101/D3)
The world's largest open-face
mine is situated in the Oquirrh
Mountains 40 km (25 miles)
southwest of the city. Miners have
already dug down 800 m
(2,640 ft) to achieve annual yields
of 20,000 metric tons (19,700

tonnes) of copper ore. *Observation
platform and Visitor Center*

Great Salt Lake   (100/C2)
The biggest lake in the American
West is actually an inland sea: its
salinity is as much as 27 per cent,
making it six times as salty as the
oceans. Only the Dead Sea is
saltier. Despite its vast size – 150
km (94 miles) long and up to 70
km (44 miles) across – the Great
Salt Lake is shallow, at most 8 m
(26 ft) deep. Since there is no
drainage, salinity and water levels are regulated entirely by
evaporation.

The best access to the water is
via the beaches on ★ *Antelope Island,* which you can reach via a
causeway. It is a nature reserve
for buffalo. The treeless salt plain
west of the lake has long been a
mecca for car-racing aficionados:
on the *Bonneville Racetrack* on I-
80, cars with rocket-powered engines keep setting new speed
records.

Timpanogos Cave   (101/D3)
This is an elongated limestone
cavern beneath the north face of
Mount Timpanogos (3,581 m/
11,800 ft) about 50 km (31 miles)
southeast of Salt Lake City. It
boasts spectacular stalactites and
stalagmites. *A steep 2.5 km (1½
miles) long path leads to the cave entrance high above the valley; admission
charge for a three-hour guided tour: $5*

VERNAL

(101/E3) This small town (pop.
7,000) in the stony desert in the
northeastern corner of Utah
seems to be inhabited by dinosaurs: dinos decorate numerous
motels, dangle from souvenir

Zion Narrows Trail, where hikers get their feet wet

shops, fill the museums. No wonder they do, for the sedimentary rock of *Dinosaur National Monument* on the eastern fringe of town is one of the world's richest fossil beds. However, the Vernal region has a lot to offer for adventure holidays: the Green River and Yampa River gorges (1,000 m/ 3,300 ft deep) are a popular venue for white-water rafting, mountain biking and backpacking trips. You really shouldn't miss ✈/▷ *Harpers Corner* in Dinosaur National Monument and ✈/▷ *Red Canyon Overlook* in *Flaming Gorge National Recreation Area*, which stretch from north of Vernal deep into the heart of Wyoming.

MUSEUMS

Dinosaur Quarry

The Visitor Center at Dinosaur National Monument houses a unique museum: a 100 m (330 ft)-long rock wall reveals dozens of dinosaur skeletons that have been left in situ to form a natural relief. *Daily 8 am–4.30 pm, in summer 8 am–7 pm; Admission: $5, about 25 km (16 miles) northeast of Vernal on SR 149*

Utah Field House of Natural History

Exhibitions of fossils and a prehistoric garden replete with life-sized dinos. *Daily 9 am–5 pm, in* *summer 8 am–8 pm; Admission: $2; 235 E Main St.*

HOTEL

Best Western Dinosaur Inn
A well-run chain motel in the town centre. *60 rooms; 251 E Main St.; Tel: (435) 789-2660; Fax: 789-2467; Category 2–3*

SPORTS & LEISURE

Hatch River Expeditions
Rafting through the canyons of the Green and Yampa Rivers on one-day and longer excursions. *55 E Main St.; Tel: (435) 789-4316; Fax: 789-8513*

ZION
NATIONAL PARK

(100/C6) This park is one of the southern Utah canyon region's smaller (only 595 sq km/372 sq miles) nature reserves but nonetheless it is very popular with backpackers who are looking for wilderness. At its core is the narrow Virgin River Gorge (700 m/ 2,310 ft deep). Over the past 13 million years the river has carved spectacularly steep walls out of the limestone and deep red Navajo sandstone of the Markagunt Plateau. Mormon pioneers named the valley after the heavenly Kingdom of Zion and gave many of the rock towers biblical names.

The scenery is particularly beautiful on ⊷ *Scenic Drive* in autumn when the mountain aspen leaves turn glowing yellow. If water levels are low, this is the time for taking the two-day hike through the narrow canyon called ★ *Zion Narrows* if you like hiking in canyons or one of many shorter routes like *Gateway to the Narrows Trail* or perhaps *Canyon Overlook Trail* and *Angels Landing Trail*, both leading to ⊷ lookout points high above the valley. In peak season shuttle buses leave from Zion Lodge to take visitors into the Canyon.

RESTAURANTS

Bit 'n Spur Saloon
⊼ Beer joint with restaurant and live music in the evenings. *Springdale, Zion Park Blvd.; Category 3*

Flanigan's
An elegant restaurant in the hotel of the same name serving excellent fish and game. ⊷ View of the river. *Springdale, 428 Zion Park Blvd.; Tel: (435) 772-3244; Category 2–3*

HOTELS

Canyon Ranch Motel
Good accommodation, 22 rooms in log cabins near the park entrance. *Springdale, 668 Zion Park Blvd.; Tel: (435) 772-3357; Fax: 772-3057; Category 2–3*

Zion Park Inn
Modern hotel with a pool and a restaurant with lots of ambience, the *Switchback Grill. 120 rooms; Springdale, 1215 Zion Park Blvd.; Tel: (435) 772-3200; Fax: 772-2449; Category 2*

INFORMATION

Zion National Park
Visitor Center, park entrance. *Postal address: Springdale, UT 84767; Tel: (435) 772-3256*

World-class art and fine cuisine

The Southwest's least known city is an attractive blend of Western ambience, ancient pueblos and lonely desert

Some Americans think New Mexico is somewhere in Central America. This large state (315,000 sq km/197,000 sq miles) is an unknown quantity in its own country. Small wonder, then, that European travellers overlook New Mexico when planning holiday itineraries in the Southwest. This is a great mistake because the sparsely populated 47th US state boasts superb, unspoilt scenery and overwhelming natural beauty. Another thing that is often forgotten is that New Mexico is surprisingly rich in history and culture.

To get a few things straight first: New Mexico is an American southwestern state bordered by the states of Arizona, Colorado and Texas, and the Republic of Mexico borders it to the south. In New Mexico only the valley of the Rio Grande, which has featured prominently in so many Westerns, is fairly densely

populated. The interior of New Mexico is sparsely dotted with derelict towns recalling the early days of the Wild West. The hot south of New Mexico is primarily sun-scorched desert. The Rocky Mountains stretch from Colorado into northern New Mexico. The Spaniards aptly called them Sangre de Cristo, 'Blood of Christ'. This remote mountain range rises to an elevation of 4,000 m (13,200 ft).

The state's misleading name also goes back to the Spaniards, who founded some of their first settlements in North America at the foot of the mountains in the early 17th century. They called their colony on the Rio Grande Nuevo Mexico. It was ceded to the United States in 1848. Many place names originated with the early Conquistadores and numerous New Mexico families are proud of being able to trace their ancestry back to the first colonists in the region.

The descendants of the Spaniards are not the only ethnic group to have shaped New Mexico's history. For over 1,000 years Pueblo tribes have lived

The Santuario de Chimayo pilgrimage church: Spanish Conquistador legacy in New Mexico

along the Rio Grande. Moreover, they have retained their ancient culture, rituals and ceremonial dances. The pueblo architecture, with its famous style based on reddish brown, sundried adobe bricks, has been taken up in all modern cities across the whole state. The white American settlers managed to leave their mark in New Mexico too: desperadoes like Billy the Kid shot their way into the Wild West legend. In the 1920s Route 66 was built, and, not long afterwards, the first atomic bomb was set off in New Mexico.

This blend of cultures, which have enriched each other, has created a unique way of life, indigenous art and the fiery hot dishes featured in New Mexican cuisine. The regional culture, unspoilt natural beauty and the 'desert light', have attracted artists like Georgia O'Keeffe to New Mexico. More and more people are moving to the state or visiting it. Once you've been to New Mexico, you'll be enthralled by it. The state motto is, aptly, *Land of Enchantment* and enchanting it is.

ACOMA PUEBLO

(108/A3) ★ One of the earliest and finest pueblos in the Southwest, 'Sky City', built by the Acoma tribe, is 110 m (363 ft) high above the desert on a very steep 〰️ mesa. Guided tours to the pueblo, built as early as AD 1150, leave from the Visitor Center at the foot of the mesa (= table mountain). The pueblo's biggest building is the Mission church of San Esteban del Rey, begun in 1629. Traditional Acoma pottery, with distinctive white and black linear decoration, is sold at stands. *In summer daily 8 am–7 pm, otherwise 8 am–4.30 pm; Admission: $6*

ALAMOGORDO

(108/C4) This smallish town (pop. 28,000) at the foot of the looming Sacramento Mountains (3,000 m/ 9,900 ft) in the hot south of New Mexico became world-famous on 16 July 1945 when the atomic age was born. To the northwest, on the vast *White Sands Missile Range*, US Army scientists tested the first atomic bomb. Today the city of Alamogordo still lives from the

MARCO POLO SELECTION: NEW MEXICO

Winter wonderland? The dunes of White Sands are of gypsum sand

rocket-building and aeronautic industries as well as the extensive runways and landing strips for Space Shuttles.

MUSEUM

Space Center
Exhibitions, planetarium laser shows and films on the history of rocket-building and aeronautics shown in a gigantic Omnimax cinema. *In summer daily 9 am–6 pm, otherwise 5 pm; Admission: $6; on US 70/54*

HOTEL

Best Western Desert Aire
Pleasant and well run, belongs to a motel chain. The quieter of the 100 rooms are situated in the central tract. *1021 S White Sands Blvd.; Tel: (505) 437-2110; Fax: 437-1898; Category 3*

SURROUNDING AREA

Ruidoso   (108/C4)
It's incredible to see how different the scenery and climate are when you drive up into the Sacramento Mountains not far from Alamogordo. The little resort town of Ruidoso on the edge of the Mescalero reservation is set in cool green pine forests. In summer, hiking trails, a horse museum and horse racing are welcome distractions and in winter you can ski here.

White Sands
National Monument   (108/B5)
★ The desert basin known as *Tularosa Valley* west of Alamogordo is a mecca for photographers, amateurs and professionals alike. Strange mobile dunes, some 20 m (66 ft) high, of white gypsum sand cover 600 sq km (375 sq miles). From the *Visitor Center* a road leads 13 km (8 miles) up into the dunescape, which looks like a valley of snowdrifts.

ALBUQUERQUE

(108/B2) New Mexico's biggest city (pop. 385,000) and its sprawling suburbs fill a plateau at the foot of the *Sandia Mountains.* The growth of the nuclear power and computer industries and the presence of a major university have turned what was once a trading post into a modern, high-tech hub. The city's long history (Albuquerque was founded in 1706 by the Spaniards and was named after the Spanish viceroy) can still be recognized in some early adobe buildings in the *Old Town* on the Rio Grande. Around the lovely plaza, you'll find a Mission church built in 1793, *San Felipe de Neri,* and museums, restaurants and galleries selling Native American jewellery. Do venture on a trip in a gondola all the way up 3,158 m (10,420 ft)-high ◁▷ *Sandia Peak* above the city and — recommended for children — visit the natural history *Biopark* along the Rio Grande.

MUSEUMS

Albuquerque Museum
Four hundred years of Spanish settlement history come alive here. *In summer daily tours through the Old Town; Tues–Sun 9 am–5 pm; Admission free; 2000 Mountain Rd. NW*

Indian Pueblo Cultural Center
This museum run by Native Americans and dedicated to the culture of the New Mexico Pueblo tribes also serves as an art market. Ceremonial dancing at weekends. Restaurant serves Native American food. *Daily 9 am–5.30 pm; Admission: $3; 2401 12th St. NW*

New Mexico Museum of Natural History & Science
Big exhibitions on the state's geology and natural history, including life-size dinosaurs. *Daily 9 am–5 pm; Admission: $5.25; 1801 Mountain Rd. NW*

RESTAURANTS

Café Oceana
This is a popular bistro specializing in excellent seafood dishes: fresh fish is flown in daily. *1414 Central Ave. SE; Tel: (505) 247-2233; Category 2–3*

Monte Vista Fire Station
Elegant restaurant in a restored fire station built in the pueblo style. Lively ⊕ bar on the top floor. *3201 Central Ave. NE; Tel: (505) 255-2424; Category 2*

Yesterdave's Bar & Grill
Lots of ⚲ 1950s nostalgia served with gigantic portions. The restaurant also boasts its own oldtimer museum. *10601 Montgomery St. NE; Tel: (505) 293-0033; Category 3*

HOTELS

Club House Inn
Good, moderately priced inn near the highway, but quiet. Good service. *154 rooms; 1315 Menaul Blvd. NE; Tel: (505) 345-0010; Fax: 344-3911; Category 2–3*

La Hacienda Grande
This 250-year-old ranch in a suburb just north of town is now a delightfully historic B & B. *6 rooms; Bernalillo, 21 Baros Lane; Tel: (505) 867-1887; Fax: 867-4621; Category 2*

INFORMATION

Albuquerque Convention & Visitors Bureau
Info kiosk in Old Town. *Postal address: P.O. Box 26866, Albuquerque, NM 87125; Tel: (505) 842-9918; Fax: 247-9101*

SURROUNDING AREA

Pueblos (108/B2)

North of Albuquerque, in the Rio Grande Valley, there are Native American pueblos, such as *San Felipe, Santo Domingo, Zia* and *Cochiti,* whose inhabitants have always been famous for pottery making. You can buy ceramics decorated with the distinctive tribal patterns at trading posts and small galleries, sometimes even directly from the makers. However, there is a great deal more you shouldn't miss; you'll have to inquire at the Visitors Bureau in Albuquerque or Santa Fe about Native American festivals at which the Pueblos perform their very colourful, traditional, ✪ ceremonial dances.

CARLSBAD CAVERNS NATIONAL PARK

(109/D5) Hidden deep in the Guadalupe Mountains in the southeastern corner of New Mexico are the New World's most magnificent caverns. The *Big Room,* the biggest cave, stretches for 550 m (1,800 ft) and its ceiling is up to 77 m (250 ft) high. It took the slightly acidic ground water about 3 million years to erode the limestone of a petrified coral reef in these vast caverns. You can explore about 5 km (3 miles) of the cave system, which is quite cool (13°C/55°F) and partly illuminated in glowing colour by spotlights, on safely roped paths. If you want a rather longer tour, walk through the natural cave entrance and take the lift down into the very heart

of the labyrinth, where two shorter tours begin. Hundreds of thousands of bats add enormously to the caverns' attraction. They aestivate in a side chamber of the caverns and you may be lucky enough to watch them fly out in a swelling, dusky cloud at sunset.

CHAMA

(108/B1) An old silver-mining town in the remote north of New Mexico, Chama is now a popular venue for steam-engine fans: from here the historic trains of the *Cumbres & Toltec Scenic Railroad,* which transported silver ore a century ago, chug to the old mines they once served, *Osier* and *Antonito* in the Colorado mountains. *To book day trips: Tel: (505) 756-2151*

RESTAURANT

High Country Restaurant

Mexican food and thick steaks as well as a great Western saloon. *On the SR 17 into town from the south; Tel: (505) 756-2384; Category 2–3*

FARMINGTON

(108/A1) This town (pop. 34,000) on the eastern borders of the large Navajo reservation can hardly compete with its attractions. Farmington is mainly an Indian trading centre and also a good point of departure for trips to Native American ruins and the surrounding country, for instance to the 500 m (1,650 ft)-high volcanic monolith called *Shiprock,* which, as legend has it, was once a giant bird that brought the ancestors of the Navajo tribe into the territory. Or to the *Bisti Badlands,* a bizarre wilderness of eroded rock south of town. In the suburb of Aztec, east of town, the *Aztec Ruins National Monument* is a ruined Anasazi settlement dating from AD 1150, which has been surprisingly well preserved. Well worth seeing: the large restored kiva, a subterranean ritual chamber. Also noteworthy are the trading posts on US 550 west of town, which have been selling blankets and silver jewellery for 100 years.

SURROUNDING AREA

Chaco Culture National Historical Park (108/A1)

A dusty gavel road runs across the remote plateau south of Farmington to Chaco Canyon. A thousand years ago one of the most important Anasazi settlements flourished here. The ruins of 13 pueblo complexes, for example *Pueblo Bonito* and *Casa Rinconada,* can still be seen here on the broad bed of the canyon, where some pueblos had hundreds of rooms. *Visitor Center*

GALLUP

(107/F2) Gallup wouldn't take a beauty prize but it is a typical town where truckers stop off. It still retains a 1950s flavour. The town (pop. 20,000) sprawls for miles along the old part of Route 66, a chain of motels, filling stations and flickering neon signs. Western shops, saddlers and fodder wholesalers as well as a host of bars indicate that Gallup is the nearby Navajo reservation's primary trading post. At trading posts and pawnshops along the road you'll find a wide selection of wares and silver jewellery.

RESTAURANT

Earl's

A classic coffee shop on Route 66, this one opened in 1947. *1400 E Hwy. 66; Tel: (505) 863-4201; Category 3*

HOTEL

El Rancho

John Wayne and many other Western stars have slept in this building since it was errected in 1937. Fine old lobby. The 72 rooms are modest but spanking clean. *1000 E Hwy. 66; Tel: (505) 863-9311; Fax: 722-5917; Category 2*

SURROUNDING AREA

El Morro National Monument (107/F3)

The steep sandstone wall of *Inscription Rock* an hour's drive southeast of Gallup reads like a 'Who's Who' of the men who have passed by. Since 1600 all conquerors have immortalized themselves on its face. There's a path leading up the rock to the ancient ruins of ☜ *Atsinna Pueblo,* which was inhabited by Native Americans until 1275.

Zuni Pueblo (107/F2)

At first sight, the biggest New Mexico pueblo looks just like any small town. However, behind the houses stand traditional Zuni clay ovens. Trading posts sell jewellery and on holidays ceremonial dances are performed by Native Americans wearing impressive masks. Noteworthy: the colourful interior of the Mission church at the centre of the pueblo.

LAS VEGAS

(108/C2) Still a small Wild West town (pop. 15,000) on the old Santa Fe Trail, which should not be confused with the more famous Nevada city, Las Vegas, New Mexico, was notorious 120 years ago as a rough place. Many a gunslinger's life ended here on the gallows. Around the *Old Town Plaza* many historic buildings have been preserved, most of them in the Victorian style of the late 19th century.

SANTA FE

(108/C2) Quirky cafés and superb restaurants, lovely adobe buildings and outstanding museums – New Mexico's capital is by far the most delightful and popular city in the state. Founded in 1609 by the Spaniards, it vies with St Augustine, Florida, for the

honour of being the oldest city in the US. At first a mere village at the foot of the Sangre de Cristo Mountains, Santa Fe was the centre of Spanish colonial power and later a trading outpost at the end of the Santa Fe Trail, famous from so many Westerns. In recent decades the city (pop. 60, 000) has grown into a mecca for New Age prophets, artists and well-heeled drop-outs. With over 200 art galleries, Santa Fe is second only to New York as a major US art centre.

SIGHTS

The heart of the old town, which is entirely in the Mexican-Indian adobe style, is the plaza with the Palace of the Governors, built in 1609. Around it are the most important attractions: in Johnson Street the new *O'Keeffe Museum,* in San Francisco Street the Art Deco (1920) *La Fonda Hotel* and the neo-Romanesque *St. Francis Cathedral* (dating from 1884). On the Old Santa Fe Trail, a building recalling the Paris Sainte-Chapelle, the *Loretto Chapel* as well as the doughty *San Miguel Mission*

Tortillas and fajitas

Mexican influence is prevalent in Arizona and New Mexico: whether you're listening to a traditional Mariachi band in a cheerfully decorated eatery or grabbing some fast food round the corner. Corn and wheat tortillas are always served: rolled and filled with cheese, meat and salad as *enchiladas* and *burritos* or deep fried as *tacos*. Tortilla chips with hot salsa are often served free with your first beer. Mashed avocado *(guacamole)*, sour cream and fried beans *(frijoles)* are, with hot chilis (the really fiery kind: *jalapeños*), the classic accompaniment to Mexican food. You shouldn't miss sampling *fajitas*, shredded roast meat with onions and chilis, served piping hot and eaten rolled in the tortillas of your choice.

dating from 1610. You should walk through the most interesting quarter around *Guadalupe Street*, with studios and art galleries that are beginning to outstrip the Canyon Road establishment.

MUSEUMS

MUSEUMS

New Mexico State Museums
New Mexico hoards and displays its cultural treasures in four large public museums: the venerable *Palace of the Governors* on the plaza is dedicated primarily to colonial history; next door to it the *Museum of Fine Arts* shows modern art from the Southwest. On the Camino Lejo south of the city are the *Museum of Indian Arts and Culture* and the *Museum of International Folk Art*. All four museums are open: *Tues–Sun 10 am–5 pm; Admission: $5*

Wheelwright Museum
Lovely hand-woven textiles and modern Navajo art. *Mon–Sat 10 am–5 pm, Sun 1 pm–5 pm; Admission free; 704 Camino Lejo*

RESTAURANTS

Geronimo's
This rather elegant place to dine serves superb Southwest cuisine. Small patio. Frequented by people from the art scene. *724 Canyon Rd.; Tel: (505) 982-1500; Category 1*

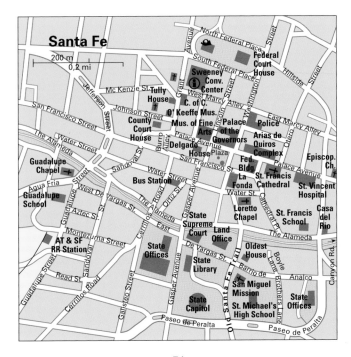

Modern art in historic houses: Canyon Road in Santa Fe

Pasqual's
A cosy bistro in the Southwestern style with excellent food. Good breakfasts. *121 Don Gaspar; Tel: (505) 983-9340; Category 2*

Tomasita's
Red-hot burritos and scrumptious fajitas in the old train station. *500 S Guadalupe St.; Tel: (505) 893-5721; Category 3*

Zia Diner
⚘ Trendy and popular with young people; serves New Mexican cuisine. Good salads and light snacks. *326 S Guadalupe St.; Tel: (505) 988-7008; Category 3*

SHOPPING

Around the *Plaza* you'll find craft and souvenir shops, some of which sell high-quality Native American jewellery. You can buy directly from the artists themselves under the arcades of the *Palace of the Governors* on the plaza. The best art galleries are along ★ *Canyon Road* on the east side of town; for jewellery, *the Silver Sun Gallery (656 Canyon Rd.);* for ceramics and textiles the *Morning Star Gallery (513 Canyon Road).*

HOTELS

Bishop's Lodge
Once the country residence of the Bishop of Santa Fe, with lovely gardens and nestled in the outlying hills. *74 rooms; Bishop's Lodge Rd.; Tel: (505) 983-6377; Fax: 989-8739; Category 1*

El Rey Inn
Comfortable motel in the adobe style, rooms with open fireplace. *86 rooms; 1862 Cerrillos Rd.; Tel: (505) 982-1931; Fax: 989-9249; Category 2–3*

Grant Corner Inn
B & B in an attractive Victorian house near the plaza. A lovely, small garden. *12 rooms; 122 Grant Ave.; Tel: (505) 983-6678; Category 2*

Hilton of Santa Fe

Not just your usual impersonal hotel but a building in Western style. Luxurious casitas in a small garden. *158 rooms; 100 Sandoval St.; Tel: (505) 988-2811; Fax: 986-6439; Category 1-2*

ENTERTAINMENT

For music lovers: don't forget tickets to the *Santa Fe Opera*, a spectacular building by Frank Lloyd Wright for enthusiates of open-air opera (performances in July/August), *Tel: (505) 986-5900*. Jazz and other live music with a long, cool drink at the lobby bar of the *La Fonda* and in the Spanish restaurant ◈ *El Farol* (*808 Canyon Rd.*)

INFORMATION

Santa Fe Visitors Bureau

201 W Marcy St., Santa Fe, NM 87501; Tel: (505) 984-6760; Fax: 984-6679

SURROUNDING AREA

Bandelier National Monument/ Los Alamos (108/B2)

In *Frijoles Canyon,* about 80 km (50 miles) northwest of Santa Fe, prehistoric Indian tribes gouged spacious cliff dwellings out of the canyon walls. A 2 km (1½ mile)-long path leads from the Visitor Center to the most important cliff dwellings. Stop at *Los Alamos* on the way back, where US atomic energy research was kept top secret for so long. Many laboratories in 'Atomic City' are still closed to the public, but in the *Bradbury Science Museum (15th St./Central Ave.)* you'll learn something

about the work done by Robert Oppenheimer and his successors.

Chimayo (108/C1)

The church of the *Santuario de Chimayo* has been a famous place of pilgrimage on the 'High Road to Taos', the old Spanish trade route between Santa Fe and the north, since 1816. After visiting the church, the patio of *Rancho de Chimayo* is a place where you can enjoy a break and superb New Mexican cuisine. There are more old Spanish villages nearby, such as *Truchas* or *Las Trampas* and Indian pueblos like *Picuris,* to discover.

SILVER CITY

(**108/A5**) A classic mining town (pop. 10,000) in the remote south of New Mexico, Silver City is notorious for being the birthplace of Billy the Kid. Several vast open-face mining pits in the area attest to the presence of rich copper-ore lodes. The town has definitely seen better days although it does have a university, which boasts a really outstanding archaeological museum.

SURROUNDING AREA

Gila Cliff Dwellings National Monument (108/A4)

Isolated ruins north of Silver City are all that is left of the mysterious Mogollon culture, which, like that of the Anasazi, vanished almost without trace about AD 1280. A labelled trail leads to the five cliff settlements in the park, where a treasure trove of magnificent pottery was found. *Visitor Center*

Shakespeare Ghost Town (107/F5)
New Mexico's finest ghost town is situated near Lordsburg south of Silver City. In 1870 thousands of silver prospectors poured into what was then a boom town. Billy the Kid washed dishes here. *Open to the public over the 2nd weekend of each month or by appointment: Tel: (505) 542-9034*

TAOS

(108/C3) Indian pueblos, Spanish colonial outposts, artist colonies that have attracted celebrities such as D.H. Lawrence and Georgia O'Keeffe; this tiny town (pop. 4,000) at the foot of the Sangre de Cristo Mountains has seen it all. By turning into an attractive blend of cultures, it has evolved into one of New Mexico's most popular holiday resorts. The historic plaza at the heart of town is surrounded by old adobe buildings. The side streets are full of artists' studios and art galleries. You can visit exhibitions showing the work of artists who once lived in Taos or actually see the houses lived in by famous artists: the *Ernest Blumenschein Home,* in *Fechin House* and in the *Millicent Rogers Museum.* Also noteworthy is the museum in the *Kit Carson Home,* where the famous scout lived, and the Spanish church, begun in 1710, of *San Francisco de Asis* in suburban Ranchos de Taos.

SIGHTS

Taos Pueblo
★ The five-storey Taos Pueblo, which is 800 years old, is still inhabited by Native Americans, many of whom live without TV or even electricity in the old adobe buildings. Ceremonial dancing in June and late September. *Daily 8 am–4.30 pm; Admission: $1; photo fees: $5; northern fringe of Taos*

RESTAURANTS

Doc Martin's
The 'in' place to frequent, the Taos Inn is a protected historic monument. The cuisine is classic New Mexican. *125 Paseo del Pueblo Norte; Tel: (505) 758-1977; Category 1–2*

Jacquelina's
An elegant but cosy place to dine south of the city, serving excellent New Mexican food. *1541 Paseo del Pueblo Sur; Tel: (505) 751-0399; Category 2*

Michael's Kitchen
❀ A rustic classic: American home cooking in a typical coffee shop ambience. *304 C Paseo del Pueblo Norte; Tel: (505) 758-4178; Category 3*

HOTELS

El Pueblo Lodge
A welcoming adobe-style motel in the north of town. *78 rooms; 412 Paseo del Pueblo Norte; Tel: (505) 758-8700; Fax: 758-7321; Category 2–3*

Inn on La Loma Plaza
An old adobe hacienda building in a quiet setting on the edge of Old Town. Beautifully restored with all modern amenities and furnished in Southwest style. *7 rooms; 315 Ranchitos Rd.; Tel: (505) 758-1717; Fax: 751-0155; Category 1–2*

Remote valleys, lofty mountains

Gold prospectors were the first to come to Colorado; now the Rocky Mountain state is a magnet for bikers, hikers and skiers

Political boundaries do not follow the lie of the land; consequently only the southwestern corner of Colorado belongs to the classic Southwest, desert country with rugged, red terrain. Colorado, on the contrary, is the Rocky Mountain state. The majestic mountain chain forms the continental divide, a watershed that nearly stretches from Canada to Mexico in the south.

Some peaks of the Rockies are higher than 4,000 m (13,200 ft). The entire state of Colorado lies at an average elevation of over 2,000 m (6,600 ft) above sea level. What most Europeans do not realize, is that the Colorado Rockies are far to the south of the Alps, on the same latitude as southern Spain so that the timber-line lies at over 3,500 m (11,550 ft), where Alpine meadows and bare rock begin in the Rockies. Most Colorado mountain resorts are at an elevation of 2,500 m (8,250 ft)

or even 3,000 m (9,900 ft) above sea level. You'll notice how high up you are when you start to huff and puff while hiking or simply climbing stairs.

The proximity of the Rockies, snow-capped until late spring, to the canyons and red monoliths of the Colorado Plateau makes for fascinating contrasts, which you can enjoy on a trip through the Southwest. A day's drive from Moab or Santa Fe will find you high up in the Rockies. Behind you are deserts, canyons and pueblos and around you is the crisp coolness (even in midsummer) of Rocky Mountain valleys studded with flowers, verdant ranch pastures and picturesque Victorian mining towns, an ideal place for backpacking in the mountains, exploring the Rockies on horseback or mountain biking. Colorado has yet another treat in store for you: in October, warm Indian summer days make mountain aspens and birches glow in fiery autumn colours.

The pioneers found the Rockies an almost insurmountable barrier to the plains and desert country on the other side. How-

Indian summer in Maroon Bells Valley near Aspen: aspens turn to gold in late September

MARCO POLO SELECTION: COLORADO

1 **Aspen**
The stars' resort of choice (page 82)

2 **Idlespur Brewery**
Venison steaks and fresh draught beer in a tiny Western town (page 83)

3 **Mesa Verde National Park**
Mysterious ruined cities of an ancient Indian civilisation (page 87)

4 **Trail Ridge Road**
Colorado's most beautiful scenic highway (page 87)

ever, from 1860, gold and silver prospectors succeeded in penetrating further into the mountain fastnesses to discover vast wealth. They left a legacy of Wild West towns that still recall those rough early days. Many towns are now popular holiday resorts with attractively restored buildings as hotels and dude ranches as well as ski lifts and a network of hiking and biking trails through the mountains.

The Rockies are 'in', as the large number of people who have chosen to move here in recent years shows. Young people and families are glad to turn their backs on crowded California and move to Colorado with its bracing mountain air, vast variety of leisure activities and attractive lifestyle. Still, the state (270,000 sq km/169,000 sq miles) has not yet reached capacity: its population has only just reached 4 million.

ASPEN/VAIL

(102/B4) These famous Rocky Mountain ski resorts in the heart of Colorado are about 50 km (31 miles) apart. The fabulous powder snow on the slopes at these fashionable resorts attracts both Hollywood stars and well-heeled European skiers. A really elegant town, ★ Aspen was once a mining town although Vail, on the other hand, is a modern ski resort designed and built along Alpine lines. During the summer many festivals are held here and visitors to them can explore the surrounding mountain country on hiking trails such as the lovely *Maroon Bells* near Aspen.

COLORADO SPRINGS

(103/D4) Despite a population explosion, this town (pop. 300, 000), founded as a health resort in 1871, has retained its restful quality. Its beautiful location on the sunny eastern slopes of the Rockies, nature reserves like ⚜ *Garden of the Gods* with its grotesque red rock formations, attractive Wild West towns like nearby *Manitou Springs* and beautifully tended golf courses make Colorado Springs a popular holiday venue. Its attractions include the Western museum *Pro-Rodeo Hall of Fame* and the impressive architecture of the *Cadet Chapel* at the US Air Force Academy north of the city.

HOTEL

The Broadmoor
Elegantly traditional at the foot of Cheyenne Mountain. Golf, tennis. *704 rooms; 1 Lake Ave.; Tel: (719) 634-7711; Fax: 577-5700; Category 1*

SURROUNDING AREA

Pikes Peak   (102/C4)
At 4,300 m (14,200 ft), Pikes Peak is one of the country's most famous mountains. Besides, it's convenient for tourists. A funicular railway runs from Manitou Springs to the top and there is even a hair-raisingly twisty scenic highway all the way up to the top.

CRESTED BUTTE

(102/B4) A former mining town (pop. 900) with lots of atmosphere at an elevation of 3,000 m (9,900 ft) in the heart of the Rockies, Crested Butte has become a mecca for mountain bikers in recent years. A good network of trails, utilizing old mining roads and pioneer trails, takes you through the mountains. During *Fat Tire Bike Week* in July each year, thousands of bikers meet in streets lined with Victorian houses. In winter, too, there's a lot going on here; that's the season for skiers to enjoy, *Mount Crested Butte* with magnificent powder snow for months on end.

RESTAURANT

Idlespur Brewery
★ Rustic steak house with beer from its own brewery. *Elk Ave.; Tel: (970) 349-5026; Category 2–3*

DENVER

(102/C3) Colorado's capital has long outgrown its rough begin-

Major city at the foot of the Rockies: Denver, Colorado's capital

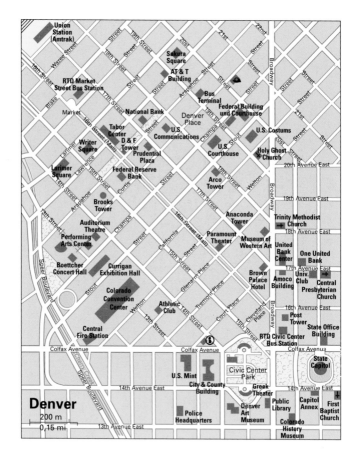

Denver
200 m
0.15 mi

nings as a Wild West boom town founded on Cherry Creek in 1858. Glittering skyscrapers, which are the mark of every big, prosperous city, shape the downtown skyline. Around the city extensive suburbs have grown right up into the foothills of the Rockies. Today, Denver and its suburbs have a population of nearly 2 million. The *Mile High City*, so called because it is situated at an elevation of 1,600 m (5,200 ft) on the eastern

slopes of the Rockies, now lives on high-tech, transport and energy industries. A dry, sunny climate, the proximity of high mountains and many parks make Denver one of the best US cities to live in.

The inner city is dominated by the golden dome, sited on a small hill, the *State Capitol* (observation platform), and, in front, the broad *Civic Center Park,* and next to it the *Colorado History Museum* tells the story of the pioneers in the Rockies; here the historic *US Mint* issues 5 billion coins a year (guided tours). North of the Civic Center Park the *16th Street Mall* begins, an attractive and popular pedestrian zone with lots of shops and cafés that runs through the heart of the city. At the northwest end of the Mall, *Larimer Square,* Denver's Old Town, boasts some of the best restaurants in the US and lively bars, great in the evening.

MUSEUMS

Denver Art Museum
A six-storey building that looks like a crenellated castle with embrasures and merlons. Inside, Native American and modern art, is exhibited. *Tues–Sat 10 am– 5 pm, Sun 12–5 pm; Admission: $4.50; 100 W 14th Ave.*

Denver Museum of Natural History
Large exhibits and models of the geology, flora and fauna of the Rocky Mountain region are on diplay in this vast building. *Daily 9 am–5 pm; Admission: $4.50; in City Park, 2001 Colorado Blvd.*

RESTAURANTS

The Fort
⬧ Wild West for gourmets: buffalo steaks are served in this restaurant outside Denver with beautiful views of the city. *Morrison, Hwy. 8; Tel: (303) 697-4771; Category 2*

Mel's Grill
A chic bistro with superb food in Cherry Creek, a fashionable suburb. *235 Fillmore St.; Tel: (303) 333-3979; Category 1–2*

Rocky Mountain Diner
⬧ Hearty Western fare in the centre of town: spare-ribs, buffalo stew. *800 18th St.; Tel: (303) 293-8383; Category 2–3*

SHOPPING

Cherry Creek Mall
A stylish shopping centre south of the city centre surrounded by art galleries and restaurants in the suburb of Cherry Creek. *University Blvd./E 1st Ave.*

HOTELS

Brown Palace
A grand old hotel with a superb lobby. At the heart of town. *232 rooms; 321 17th St.; Tel: (303) 297-3111; Fax: 293-9204; Category 1*

Comfort Inn Downtown
A comfortable chain hotel, in a good part of town. *229 rooms; 401 17th St.; Tel: (303) 296-0400; Fax: 297-0774; Category 2–3*

Warwick
A welcoming, moderately priced hotel on the eastern fringe of the inner city. 194 large rooms, rooftop pool. *1776 Grant St.; Tel: (303) 861-2000; Fax: 839-8504; Category 1–2*

ENTERTAINMENT

The most trendy places to go at the moment are the bars and restaurants in *Larimer Square (Larimer St./15th St.)* as well as the those in the old warehouse district of ⬧ *Lower Downtown,* which, to a large extent has been restored and where numerous little breweries like ⚓ *Wynkoop Brewing Company (1634 18th St.)* have sprung up.

Denver Visitors Bureau
*225 W Colfax Ave., Denver, CO
80202; Tel: (303) 892-1112; Fax:
892-1636*

Boulder **(102/C3)**
✪ This lively university town an
hour's drive north of Denver is a
classic example of the American
campus town: young people on
bicycles everywhere, lots of activity in the pedestrian zone,
packed with eateries and pubs,
books and coffee shops.

Golden **(102/C3)**
An old town 20 km (12½ miles)
west of Denver, Golden nestles
right at the foot of the Rockies, a
good starting point for day trips
into the *Denver mountain parks.*
The peak of *Lookout Mountain*
is famous for the grave of the
Western hero and Pony Express
rider *Buffalo Bill* (museum).
Down below in the town you
can visit one of the world's
biggest breweries: *Coors (13th
St./Ford St.)*

DURANGO

(102/A6) During the 1880 silver
boom, the town of Durango
(pop. 13,000) was a major railway junction and supplies depot
for the mines in the San Juan
Mountains. The beautifully restored Victorian houses and rak-
ish Wild West saloons lining
Main Ave. date from that era,
greatly enhancing Durango's

A 13th-century Anasazi stone town: Cliff Palace at Mesa Verde

charm and making it a marvellous summer holiday resort. Several scenic highways fan out into the mountains and to mining centres like *Telluride, Silverton* and *Ouray.* In late August Harley-Davidson fans converge in Durango for a huge bikers' gathering.

TOURS

Durango & Silverton Narrow Gauge Railroad
A historic narrow-gauge railway with steam engines. From May to Oct. all-day excursions to Silverton (70 km/44 miles). It's definitely necessary to book tickets well in advance! *479 Main Ave.; Tel: (970) 247-2733*

HOTEL

Strater
A gold prospectors' hotel, beautifully restored. Handsome saloon. *93 rooms; 699 Main Ave.; Tel: (970) 247-4431; Fax: 259-2208; Category 1–2*

SURROUNDING AREA

Mesa Verde National Park (102/A6)
★ In the canyons on the southern slopes of a large mesa, *Mesa Verde,* about 50 km (31 miles) west of Durango the most impressive Indian ruins in the US bear witness to the sophisticated Anasazi culture, which lived here about AD 500 and built large cliff dwellings about 1200. Along the circular trails that start at the Visitor Center (museum), ◥◣ lie over 30 archaeological sites, some of them open to the public, like the *Spruce Tree Ruin* or *Balcony House* — guided

tours only — and the 217 rooms of the impressive *Cliff Palace.*

GRAND JUNCTION

(102/A4) This farming town (pop. 29,000) in the broad, here really fertile, valley of the Colorado River is famous for dinosaur finds. Some of the richest fossil beds in the Rockies draw palaeontologists to Colorado. In the attractively organized museum, *Dinosaur Valley,* in the centre of town *(4th St./Main St.)* you can even watch palaeontologists in the lab, and the *Devil's Canyon Science Center* on I-70 west of town boasts life-size reconstructions of the dinos found in the area. Moreover, this is an excellent point of departure for trips into the spectacular canyons of *Colorado National Monument* (popular venue for biking trips) west of town and into the *Black Canyon of the Gunnison National Monument* 120 km (75 miles) to the southeast.

ROCKY MOUNTAIN NATIONAL PARK

(102/C3) About 100 km (60 miles) northwest of Denver magnificent scenery awaits you in the heart of the Rockies. The most beautiful scenic highway in this 1,080 sq km (675 sq mile)-park is ★ *Trail Ridge Road,* which crosses the continental divide at an elevation of 3,713 m (12,253 ft). Side valleys with lovely mountain lakes, such as ◥◣ *Bear Lake* or *Bierstadt Lake.* Visitor Center, Camping ground and accommodation in the old resort *Estes Park* at the eastern entrance to the park.

Through canyons and desert cacti

These routes are marked in green on the map inside front flap and in the road atlas beginning on page 100

① HIGHLIGHTS OF THE CANYONS

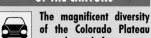

The magnificent diversity of the Colorado Plateau spreads out before you on this round trip, which will take about three weeks; the Grand Canyon and Monument Valley as well as Native American reservations and ancient ruined pueblos – a trip through superlative Wild West scenery. Along the way you'll pass many more, less well-known national parks and canyons, untouched mountain country and Wild West towns. Start from Las Vegas, Phoenix or even Los Angeles. The ideal time for this trip (3,400 km/2,125 miles) is from mid-May to early October.

After a night spent in the casinos, leaving *Las Vegas (p. 29)* may not be easy but the bracing desert air will soon clear your head. Travel north on the I-15, taking all the time you want for a detour into the superb *Valley of Fire (p. 37)* between red canyon walls, where you'll get your first taste of the natural wonders of canyon country.

Now you're not far from the Utah state line; *St. George* greets you with a huge *temple (Visitor Center)*, letting you know you're

in Mormon territory. From here SR 9 winds on to *Zion National Park (p. 67)*, the westernmost large nature reserve on the Colorado Plateau. You might want to break for a day here and stretch your legs by backpacking into the interior through wild canyon country high up on the green *Markagunt Plateau* before driving east to US 89 and one of the really great adventures en route: magnificent *Bryce Canyon National Park (p. 57)* with its delicate filigree of stone sculpture.

The next section of your itinerary on ⇘ SR 12 is a particularly scenic stretch of the Southwest: deeply fissured mesas, canyon after canyon and desert valleys wherever you look. You drive past *Boulder (p. 86)*, to cross into cool forests at an elevation of nearly 3,000 m (9,900 ft) and finally ⇘ *Boulder Mountain* before driving down into *Capitol Reef National Park (p. 58)* — superb terrain for a day's hiking among red sandstone cliffs. Another marvellous place for backpacking: the trails to *Golden Throne* and to *Hickman Arch*.

North of *Hanksville* you should make a detour on Hwy. 24 to the comically photogenic stone dwarfs in *Goblin Valley (p. 59)* just for fun and in *Green River* you can visit the *Powell River History Museum (885 E Main St.)* to learn about the history of the discoverers on the Colorado River. Then there's a short stretch of Highway I-70 before you turn south on to US 191 to *Moab (p. 59)*, home to some of the most impressive national parks and natural wonders in the US. It's advisable to book accommodation for several nights in Moab so you can explore the surrounding country on foot, mountain bike or even by raft.

Then your route follows the Colorado River on SR 128, against a superbly photogenic *rocky backdrop* of *mesas* , then eastward on the I-70 to the state of Colorado. Be sure not to miss the opportunity of taking a short excursion to a site well known from Westerns, *Fisher Valley.*

Grand Juction (p. 87) marks the northernmost point of your route. US 50 branches south here towards the town of *Montrose,* where you can detour to ❧ *Black Canyon of the Gunnison* for a spectacular surprise. For two million years the Gunnison River has cut deep (800 m/ 2,640 ft) into the volcanic ash and hard metamorphic rock to carve *Black Mesa (Visitor Center at Gunnison Point on the canyon's south rim).*

A change of scene: from the Colorado Plateau, the US 550 climbs up into the remote vastness of the *San Juan Mountains,* western outliers of the Rocky Mountains. Some Victorian mining towns dating from the 1890s boom era like *Telluride* (a short detour on SR 62/145)

for some authentic Wild West ambience. In the town of *Ouray* — yet another one-horse town — you can relax from your trip in the *thermal springs,* and in the *Bachelor-Syracuse Mine* on the edge of town you can venture into an *old mine,* which is open to the public. On the scenic ❧ *Million Dollar Highway* you cross the pass (above 3,000 m/9,900 ft) high in the *San Juan Mountains* and drive on to *Durango (p. 86).*

West of Durango you'll be confronted with an entirely different and much older cultural attraction: the celebrated ruins of *Mesa Verde (p. 87).* Less well known yet just as impressive, with a mystical stillness all their own, the ruins at *Hovenweep National Monument* , west of Cortez on the way to *Blanding (p. 56)* are a must.

Back again in the state of Utah, the road now re-enters red canyon country. A marvellous place for backpacking is *Natural Bridges National Monument;* further south at ❧ *Muley Point* you'll be amazed at the breathtaking panorama. Now you're in John Wayne country and on Western territory as you go through *Monument Valley (p. 45),* made famous by the movies, and then from *Kayenta* you can drive far into the *Navajo reservation* to *Canyon de Chelly National Monument (p. 40).*

Stony desert all the way to the horizon. On US 160/SR 98 your route runs through the most remote corners of the Navajo reservation. But then at *Page* things look really different: set in fiery red rock walls are the sapphire waters of man-made *Lake Powell (p. 45).* Time for a boat trip in the desert. Next stop: the *Grand Canyon (p. 43)*, the South-west's most famous attraction. US 180 runs straight as an arrow south across the green plateau to the south rim of the vast chasm, and the volcanic cone that is *Flagstaff (p. 42)*, where you'll certainly want to hike to the Indian ruins in *Walnut Canyon, is* something you shouldn't miss.

From Flagstaff US 89A winds through the beautiful mazes of *Oak Creek Canyon* to the art galleries of *Sedona (p. 49)* before climbing up into the mountains and Wild West *Jerome (p. 50)*. Your route continues north across the mountains and then westward on I-40.

On the last stage of your trip you can enjoy a classic piece of Americana, at least as far as roads are concerned: the fabulous *Route 66,* from *Seligman* and on through desert valleys and rundown towns like *Peach Springs* to *Kingman (p. 45)*. From there it's only about three hour's drive back full circle to Las Vegas.

② COWBOYS AND CACTI: THE SOUTH OF ARIZONA

 A short round trip lasting 8 days through the hot south – ideal for the winter months but manageable in summer in an air-conditioned car. Miles and miles of cactus and one-horse towns straight out of your favourite Westerns line your route through the desert. Take this 1,300 km/800 mile-long trip in March and April when the cactus is in bloom.

The best place to get in the mood for the desert is in *Phoenix (p. 47)*, if you visit the *Desert Botanical Garden,* where you can familiarize yourself with all the regional species of cactus. From there you take off into the desert, following the edge of the city along the bumpy *Apache Trail (p. 49)* (if you've hired a caravan [US: trailer] you'd be better off on US 89/60).

In the silver-mining town of *Globe* the museum of the *Besh-Ba-Gowah Archeological Park* is informative on Salado Indian culture. Along Hwy. 77, you'll pick up the trail of white pioneer settlers: huge ore tips left from the mines in the Pinal Mountains, where both silver and copper have been mined for well over a century.

Via *Oracle* with its futuristic-looking research complex, *Biosphere 2 (p. 53)*, you drive on to *Tucson (p. 51)*, where the superb cactus forests of *Saguaro National Park (p. 51)* invite further investigation on foot. Then you take the I-10 through empty desert, stopping on the way to look at *Kartchner Caverns* near *Benson* and in *Dragoon* the large *Native American museum of* the Amerind Foundation.

It'll get even lonelier after *Willcox* on SR 185, which turns south to the *Chiricahua Mountains* where Apache warriors once ambushed unwary settlers. The virtually inaccessible canyons and rocky labyrinths of ⚜ *Chiricahua National Monument* are now a favourite haunt of backpackers, especially in summer when the mountain region is cool.

Via *Douglas,* a ranching town on the Mexican border, your road winds on through Wild West towns with stirringly Western names like *Bisbee (p. 40)* and *Tombstone (p. 50)*. In *Nogales*

Road Atlas of the Southwest

Please refer to back cover for an overview of this road atlas

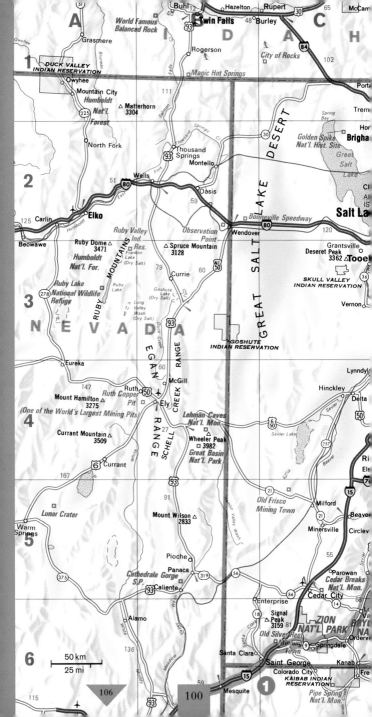

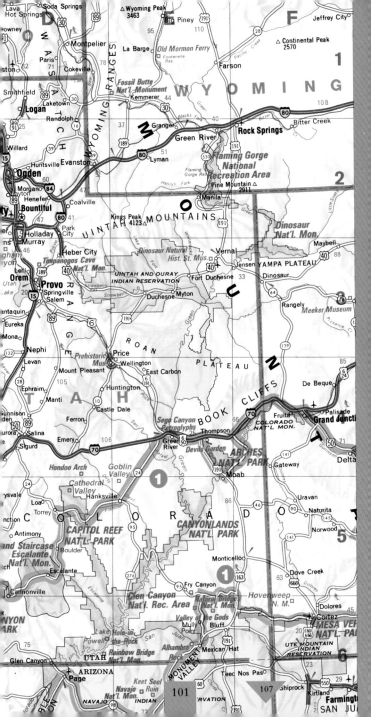

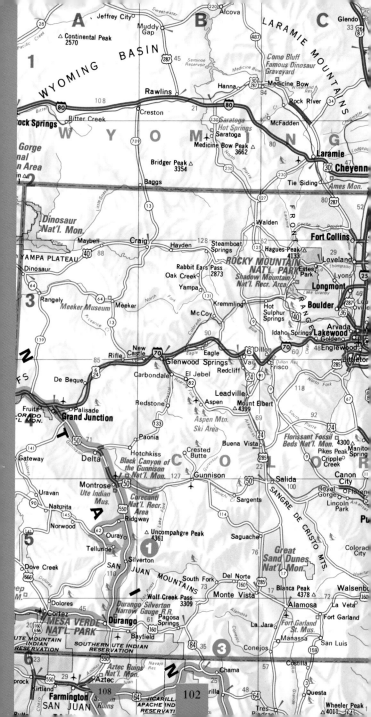

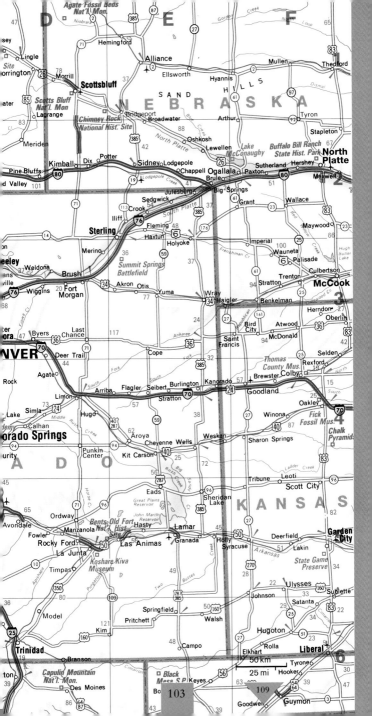

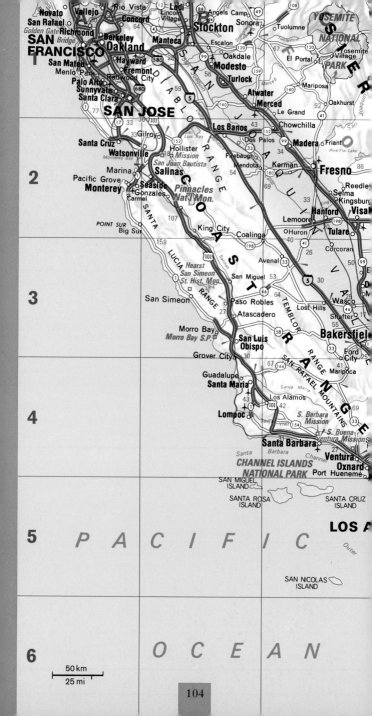

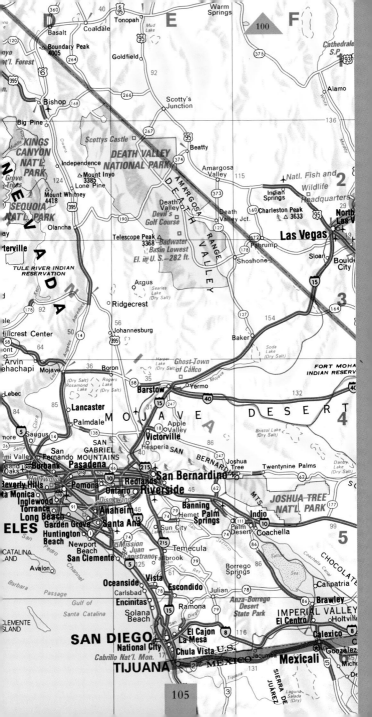

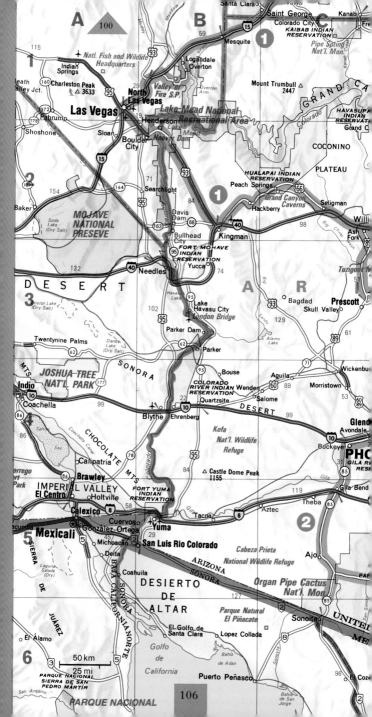

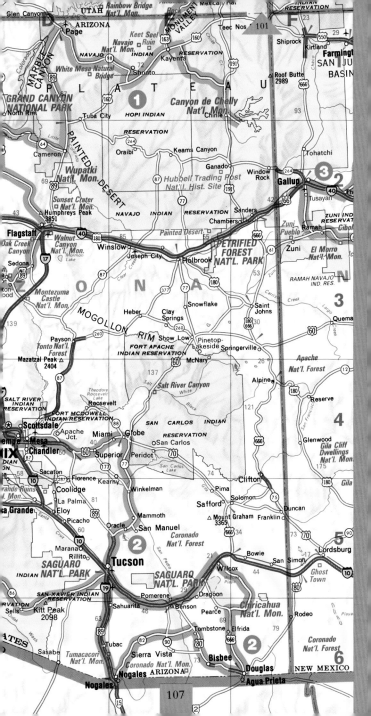

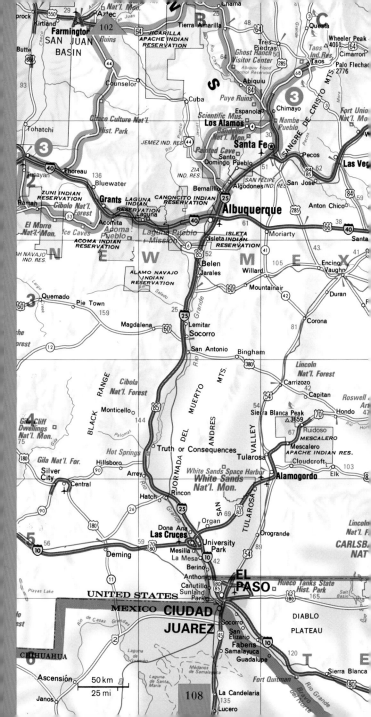

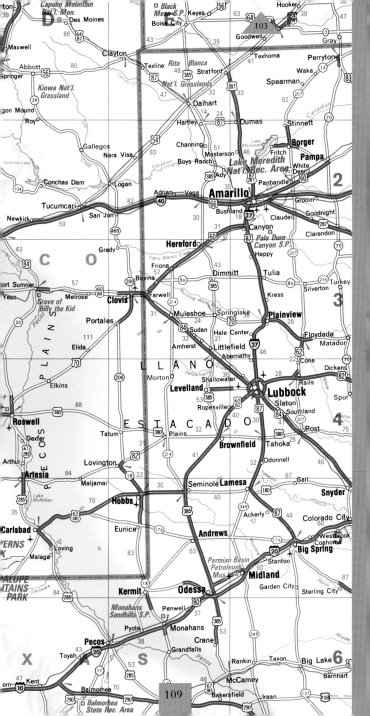

ROAD ATLAS LEGEND

German / French	Symbol	English / Spanish
Freeway (Autobahn) Freeway (Autoroute)		Freeway (Motorway) Freeway (Autopista)
Tollway (Autobahn), gebührenpflichtig Tollway (Autoroute), à péage		Tollway (Motorway) Tollway (Autopista), de peaje
Wichtige Verbindungsstrasse Route de liaison importante		Important through road Carretera de comunicación importante
Distanzen in Meilen Distances en milles	15 7 11 5	Distances in miles Distancias en millas
Interstate Highway Interstate Highway	(90)	Interstate Highway Interstate Highway
U.S. Highway U.S. Highway	(97)	U.S. Highway U.S. Highway
State and Provincial Highway State and Provincial Highway	(97)	State and Provincial Highway State and Provincial Highway
Trans-Canada-Highway Trans-Canada-Highway	🍁	Trans-Canada Highway Trans-Canada Highway
Route 66 Route 66	(66)	Route 66 Route 66
Eisenbahn Chemin de fer		Railroad Ferrocarril
Hauptstadt eines Bundesstaates Capital d'Etat fédéré	⊛	State Capital Capital de Estado Federal
Internationaler, Nationaler Flughafen Aéroport international, national	✈ +	International, National airport Aeropuerto internacional, nacional
Wintersportort Région de ski	⚲	Ski resort Deporte invernal
Höhe in Meter ü. M. Altitude en mètres	Mount Adams △ 3751	Height in meters Altitud en metros
Sehenswertes Objekt Edifice d'interêt	▫ White House	Place of interest Objeto de interés
Natursehenswürdigkeit Curiosité naturelle	Beach S.P. ▫ ▫ Lake Tahoe	Natural curiosity Curiosidad natural
Nationalpark Parc national	YOSEMITE NAT'L PARK	National Park Parque nacional
Regionalpark/Erholungsgebiet Parc regional/Zone de détente	Hells Canyon Nat'l Rec. Area	State Park/Recreation Area Parque regional/Zona de recreo
Indianerreservat Réserve d'Indiens	CROW IND. RESERVATION	Indian Reservation Reserva India
Staatsgrenze Frontière d'Etat		National frontier Frontera nacional
Bundesstaatsgrenze Limite d'Etat fédéré		State border Limite de Estado Federal

50 miles
50 km

Distances in miles

All place names, natural monuments, museums, sights to see and places to visit are included here. Page numbers in bold face refer to the main entry and numbers in italics to photos (NM = National Monument, NP = National Park, SP = State Park)

What do you get for your money?

The Southwest is certainly not cheap but for visitors from Europe, the dollar exchange rate is favourable. Flights have become cheaper in recent years; however hotels and restaurants are definitely more expensive than they were a few years ago. Nevertheless, food, clothing and many other commodities and services cost less than in most European countries.

Let's look at what your purchasing power is in the Southwest. Breakfast at a coffee shop costs about $5-$7 although you'll have to pay between $10 and $15 at exclusive hotels. A cup of coffee costs $1.50 and a cappuccino or a Mexican coffee about $3. A hearty steak dinner with all the trimmings comes to between $20 and $25. At gourmet restaurants serving fine Southwest cuisine, you'll pay anywhere from $25 to $35 for an evening meal. A glass of American or Mexican beer costs $3 and if you must have imported bottled lager, it will set you back at least $4. A gallon of petrol (gasoline) costs $1.40 and a postcard to Europe 50 c. Admission fees to national parks range from $5 to $20 per vehicle but a year's pass valid for all parks costs only $50. Riding the trail on horseback at a dude ranch costs $40 to $50. Credit cards are accepted everywhere.

US $	UK £	Can $
1	0.59	1.55
2	1.18	3.10
3	1.77	4.65
4	2.36	6.20
5	2.95	7.75
10	5.90	15.50
15	8.85	32.25
20	11.80	31.00
30	17.70	46.50
40	23.60	62.00
50	29.50	77.50
60	35.40	93.00
70	41.30	108.50
80	47.20	124.00
90	53.10	139.50
100	59.00	155.00
200	118.00	310.00
300	177.00	465.00
400	236.00	620.00
500	295.00	775.00
750	442.50	1162.50
1000	590.00	1550.00